CROWLEY'S AP

About the author

Gerald Suster was educated at Trinity Hall, Cambridge, and has written numerous books including nine novels as well as a study of the occult ideas of Hitler, and a biography of Aleister Crowley. He was a personal friend of Israel Regardie and has had a long-standing interest in occult ideas.

CROWLEY'S APPRENTICE

The Life and Ideas of Israel Regardie

by

Gerald Suster

RIDER

LONDON SYDNEY AUCKLAND JOHANNESBURG

Rider & Co Ltd
An imprint of Century Hutchinson Ltd
Brookmount House, 62–65 Chandos Place, Covent Garden,
London WC2N 4NW

Century Hutchinson Australia (Pty) Ltd
88–91 Albion Street, Surry Hills, NSW 2010

Century Hutchinson New Zealand Ltd
PO Box 40-086, 32–34 View Road, Glenfield, Auckland 10, New Zealand

Century Hutchinson South Africa (Pty) Ltd,
PO Box 337, Bergvlei, 2012, South Africa

First published in Great Britain by Rider & Co Ltd 1989

Set in Plantin by Avocet, Bicester, Oxon

Printed and bound in Great Britain by
Guernsey Press Company Ltd

British Cataloguing in Publication Data

Suster, Gerald, *1951–*
Crowley's apprentice: the life and ideas of Israel
Regardie.
1. Occultism. Regardie, Israel, *1907–1985*
I. Title
133′.092′4

ISBN 0–7126–2937–8

Contents

	Introduction	ix
1	Adolescent Awakenings	1
2	Yoga and the Intelligent Teenager	10
3	The Approach to Magic	18
4	The Wickedest Man in the World	31
5	First Fruits	52
6	The Golden Dawn and a Poison Cloud	62
7	On the Couch	79
8	A Friend in Jesus?	93
9	Solve et Coagula	102
10	The Art of True Healing	110
11	'It's a funny old world ...'	127
12	The Occult Explosion	138
13	Light in Extension	149
14	The Sage of Sedona	160
15	Ecce Homo	181

To JAMES

Introduction

Dr Francis Israel Regardie (1907–85) is one of the most important figures in the twentieth-century development of what some have called the Western Esoteric Tradition. The elements of this tradition have their origins long before the birth of Christ; they survived during the Middle Ages, were openly revived for a time during the Renaissance and continued to exist during the Scientific Revolution, but the phrase 'Western Esoteric Tradition' normally refers to the synthesis accomplished by 'MacGregor' Mathers within the Hermetic Order of the Golden Dawn during the early 1890s. Some proceeded to explore and build upon this tradition, taking it to pastures unsuspected by Mathers. Aleister Crowley is an obvious example; and Regardie stands out too as a figure of central importance.

Earlier this year, Ms Laura Jennings, a leading representative of the Israel Regardie Foundation set up shortly before the latter's death, asked me for a brief testimony to the man's memory for the Foundation's records and possible publication. I endeavoured to oblige with the following:

When a great Magician dies, one is sure to be bored by those who loudly proclaim: 'I was his Great Disciple'. In Regardie's case, they condemn themselves for he did not have disciples; he had friends. I was proud to be one of them though it was obvious to me that he was older, more accomplished and much wiser than myself.

I first met Regardie in Los Angeles, after a correspondence on Crowley, in the Summer of 1972 and found him both impressive and delightful. I especially appreciated his kindness, his modesty and his gloriously sane and refreshing sense of humour. My return to England meant that I did not see him again until my stay in America 1981–2, which is when we became friends.

At the age of 76, his vim and vigour put many young men to

shame. He was a consistently stimulating and charming companion and I treasure the memories of staying at his lovely home in Sedona and enjoying the excellence of his hospitality. He was a man who loved life and this was reflected in the broad range of his interests; he even shared my love of Boxing. He never forced his own views on others – 'The divine Genius is within you,' he used to say, 'do it yourself' – though one could aways turn to him for sagacious advice.

I had the honour of receiving instruction from him – he was reluctant to teach though superb once he was persuaded to do so – and of witnessing his magical work. Here, his style was calm, authoritative, firm and courteous – yet the Power his Magic generated was awesome. There was a pure and shining integrity about his dedication to the Great Work and this was shown too in his impatience with pretension and inessentials. Whenever he was asked his Grade, he would reply: 'I'm a student. We're all students.' In my view, Golden Dawn Magic owes its continued survival to the tireless work of Regardie.

He was an excellent writer on Magic and Psychology and performed a lasting service by bringing these two disciplines together. His style was crisp and clear, his contents of permanent value to any seeker after Wisdom. One particularly applauds his technical innovations which gave us the Middle Pillar Ritual and the Opening by Watchtower; and *The Eye in the Triangle*, by far the finest study of Aleister Crowley. *The Complete Golden Dawn System of Magic* is of course his greatest contribution: one might call it the essential compendium of pure Magical Classicism, and all students owe Regardie a lasting debt of gratitude.

One evening when I was sitting with Regardie out on his sun-deck and we were gazing at the canyons in the distance, I asked him for the greatest piece of wisdom about life that he knew. 'Sounds banal, I know,' he replied, 'but it's a funny old world.' That was in the Summer of 1982 and in the years since then, I have found that allegedly banal statement to be Of All Truth on every plane. I can hear Regardie's voice as I am typing this. 'Oh, yes,' the old man's chuckling, 'It's a funny old world.'

The foregoing was an endeavour to summarize the essence of the matter, though obviously very much more needs to be said: hence this work. Its seed was planted in a curious way.

Back in Easter 1982, my then wife, Ann, and I were staying at Regardie's home in Sedona, Arizona. The house could be reached via an uphill road called Inspiration Drive concerning which Regardie related to us an interesting local belief. Those who had lived in Sedona for many years held that if a writer or artist walked or drove up Inspiration Drive, a creation would result. The following day, Ann and I made a point of taking the car up Inspiration Drive – after all, it is not called Inspiration Walk. I have to confess, with all due shame, that to my conscious knowledge I felt no inspiration whatsoever. However, during the brief ascent of the road, Ann became calmly convinced that one of my future projects had to be a book on Israel Regardie.

I thought about this for a time and gradually the conviction grew strongly within me that Ann was right. Therefore, when I next stayed with Regardie, I raised the matter and asked for his permission to proceed the moment I had the time and the publisher. He considered the proposal thoughtfully then responded by stating that no, he would not allow me to write a detailed account of his life.

'My life is of no interest to anybody except me,' he declared. 'No.'

I retorted that he had misunderstood and I had not clearly explained the nature of my intended approach. It was not my purpose to explore and expound the day-to-day details of his worldly existence. It was the evolution and expression of his thought which fascinated me. My goal was to study the ideas of an interesting man who honestly sought wisdom and whose writings have influenced so many; indeed, one could see this influence growing with the republication of all his works. Therefore my book would indeed give an essential outline of his life, including anything he chose to tell me for publication; but its aims were to study the progress of his thought, scrutinize the traditions and ideas presented in a form intelligible to the general reader yet satisfying to the specialist, constructively criticize these statements which are open to question and, finally, paint a portrait of a man.

Moreover there were, I argued, five vital factors. Unlike many seekers after wisdom, Regardie did not embrace a way, reject it and then rush blindly into another enthusiasm which would dominate his life until the next rejection and the succeeding embrace. As he grew, he sought to expand his knowledge and to harmonize new discoveries with all he had gained from the past. For instance, his early views on Aleister Crowley and the Golden Dawn were later altered in the light of psychology and further life experience – in my opinion, there was a great maturing – yet he always held fast to the fundamental vision of his youth.

Secondly, whereas Crowley, for example, was born with every advantage for the single-minded pursuit of hidden wisdom and saw himself as a member of an elite, Regardie had to overcome all manner of social and financial handicaps – it is testimony to his determination that he managed to undertake his quest at all – and his approach was democratic.

Thirdly, Regardie's emphasis was always on coming to the Light. This theme dominates all his writings, whatever the particular subject.

The essence of the matter was, fourthly, the story of how an ordinary boy from a poor background, with little to assist him other than his own integrity and self-educated natural intelligence, pursued the Light of Truth via various means, became an illuminated man through this persistent quest and radiated that Light to others.

Finally, the proposed work certainly required a comprehensive exposition of Regardie's concerns which would satisfy the most exacting expert; but it would be executed as a narrative of intellectual and metaphysical adventure.

Such was my proposal and this time there was no hesitation at all in Regardie's reply. Three words said everything.

'Go to it!'

1

Adolescent Awakenings

Israel Regardie, born Israel Regudy, was handicapped at birth with every social and economic disadvantage. The date was 17 November 1907 and the place was just off the Mile End Road in London's East End, in a dwelling Aleister Crowley later cruelly called 'one of the vilest slums in London'. His parents were poor Jewish immigrants and so at that time were looked down upon by one and all.

During the First World War, an elder brother enlisted in the armed forces and the recruiting sergeant mistakenly recorded the name as 'Regardie', which name the family appears to have taken for its own reasons. In August 1921 the Regardies emigrated to America and Washington, DC. There, young Israel resolved during his teenage years to become a painter and to this end attended art school in Philadelphia, Pennsylvania. Moreover, at the age of fifteen he had seen a reference to Madame Blavatsky in a book belonging to his sister. Fascinated by the name, he had looked it up, learned about her stormy life, and gone on to read Blavatsky's remarkable writings. 'From then on,' he later recalled, 'I was hooked.'

Helena Petrovna Blavatsky was born in the Ukraine in 1831, and after various wanderings and adventures, including marriage, landed in New York in 1873, proclaiming an interest in, and knowledge of, Eastern esoteric doctrines. There she met Colonel Olcott and with his assistance founded the Theosophical Society two years later: the avowed aim was the study of Hidden Wisdom. In 1878, Madame Blavatsky and Colonel Olcott sailed to India, where the Theosophical Socicty met with unexpected success. After some years of acclaim, and then a series of scandals involving allegations that Blavatsky's boasted mediumistic powers were fraudulent, she returned to Europe and England, where she died in 1891.

Madame Blavatsky habitually smoked like a chimney, drank like a fish, swore like a trooper and made love like a Cleopatra – furthermore, her chain-smoking consisted of roll-ups made from a heady mixture of tocacco and cannabis. Her successors were not even fit to carry her ash-tray. Edward Maitland was earnest but dull and Anna Kingsford was described by Aleister Crowley as 'handicapped by a brain that was a mass of putrid pulp, and a complete lack of social status, education and moral character'. However, the Theosophical Society continued to flourish until Annie Besant, a sanctimonious prig, and C. W. Leadbeater, rightly assailed by Crowley as 'a senile sodomite', succeeded in inadvertently blunting the theosophical thrust with witless proclamations, then compounded their folly by announcing that a young Indian boy, Krishnamurti, was in fact Christ returned to Earth and the World Messiah.

In the winter of 1910, Krishnamurti and his younger brother Nityananda moved into quarters adjacent to Leadbeater at the insistence of the latter. Shortly afterwards, Annie Besant had the boys taken into her care. In 1911, the father of the boys filed a law suit for the recovery of his sons and succeeded in a trial, Madras 1912, during the course of which allegations of pederasty were made against Leadbeater.

To Krishnamurti's great credit, he was inwardly moved to repudiate publicly the ridiculous role thrust upon him by his manipulating mentors and he has subsequently put in a lifetime's laudable work in unpretentiously awakening enlightenment in others. However, the fatuity of Besant and Leadbeater brought Theosophy into a richly deserved ridicule from which it has never recovered. Although the Theosophical Society is still in being, these days it is the preserve of those who prefer tepid tea to tough thought.

Yet the influence of Madame Blavatsky's astonishing works can hardly be overestimated. There has hardly been an occultist since her death who has not been affected by her ideas, whether directly or indirectly. The lady went so far as to claim that the composition of her books *Isis Unveiled* (1877) and *The Secret Doctrine* (1888) was assisted by clairvoyance, and that obscure works and quotations had suddenly appeared in obedience to her needs and desires; that she was familiar with 'the oldest book in the world', the incalculably ancient *Stanzas of Dzyan*; and that Hidden Masters were in regular communication with her person. Needless to say, these claims have been disputed, but whatever the sources of Blavatsky's inspiration, and whatever else she may have been, the woman was not a mere charlatan, for no charlatan could possibly have written her exquisite mystical masterpiece, *The Voice of The Silence*.[1]

Blavatsky's writings challenged Christianity, which she loathed, and proclaimed in its stead a Westernized Hinduism, with its attractive doctrines of reincarnation and karma. They led people to seek alternatives to the Christian religion, and to suspect the existence of non-material occult forces, as mysterious and intangible as electricity, thus preparing the way in the popular mind for future scientific investigation. Whereas Nietzsche taught that the Superman is the imminent next stage in human evolution, Blavatsky announced that Supermen already existed, that they were the Hidden Masters who inhabited Central Asia, and that they could be contacted telepathically by those who had been initiated into their mysteries. Whereas the chemists and physicists taught that there was little more to learn about a universe of matter, Blavatsky insisted that there was much more to learn about a universe of spirit, which could act upon the former. And whereas biologists taught that man evolved from the apes, Blavatsky revealed that there have been four root races before our own, which incluced the ancient civilizations of lost Lemuria and Atlantis, and that evolution has been assisted by divine kings from the stars.

Although Regardie's early enthusiasm for Blavatsky's ideas was soon tempered by further reading and a critical approach, and although he deplored the errors of Blavatsky's successors, throughout his life he continued to praise the woman and her work. It is not difficult to understand why Blavatsky's writings had such a galvanizing influence upon the adolescent

Regardie. He had hardly enjoyed an upbringing conducive to mind-expansion. In common with so many of his era – and ours – he had been brought up to believe in very narrow limitations to his future development.

The religion of his family was the strict and literal Judaism of the period. This prescribed rules for every particular mode of conduct and was severely orthodox. Those who are Jewish or part-Jewish have every valid reason for taking a proper pride in the fact;[2] and there is much to be said for the simple code enunciated by Moses in The Ten Commandments: yet so many who have undergone a traditional Judaic upbringing have subsequently condemned its suppressive nature. Regardie's early and thorough training in Hebrew would stand him in excellent stead when he came later to study the Kabbala but he early rejected the accompanying dogma of the organized religion in which he had been reared.

The essence of Judaism is that God chose the Jews to be His People and mapped out a destiny for them. Through His Prophets, the greatest of whom was Moses, He laid down Laws covering all the eventualities of the time under which His People should and must live. He led the Israelites out of captivity in Egypt, sustained them throughout their wanderings in the wilderness, brought them to victory in battle against their enemies and gave them the Promised Land, the 'land of milk and honey'. He gave them Prophets and He gave them Judges and He gave them Kings: and David the Great and Solomon the Wise are still esteemed and honoured in the memory of Mankind. Unfortunately, or so it is held, the Children of Israel rebelled against the Laws of God, and repeated punishments, such as the Babylonian Captivity, did not have the desired effect of moral and religious improvement. Eventually, the Jews were scattered by the Romans and two thousand years of intermittent but horrendous persecution followed. Jews believe, however, that in the end the Messiah will come – they hold that Jesus Christ committed blasphemy in claiming to be the Son of God – and the Chosen People will be reunited in the Promised Land, justice will be done and the Will of the Lord shall prevail.

Until that time, a devout Jew must faithfully observe the injunctions and commandments of YAHWEH Lord of Hosts. It can be argued that adherence to the Law of God in accordance with Torah (the Law) and the Talmud (the Rabbinical teachings on the law) makes of one a righteous human being. It can also be argued that it could make one self-righteous. Some of the laws must strike an observer as being out of date. For instance, the prohibition against the eating of pork made absolute sense in its time. The flesh of the desert pig could infect its human consumer with a horrible and fatal disease, so a taste for pork could result in decimation of the tribe. If Moses had rationally pointed out the health risks, this would have had as little effect as Government Health Warnings on cigarette packets; so it was necessary to make of the matter a divine rule given by God. It is difficult for a non-member of the Jewish faith to perceive the relevance of this commandment to the world of today. The present writer trusts that his Jewish readers will forgive him for this comment, though they may not forgive his subject for his oft repeated statement to his friends: 'Moses? Yes. The Jewish religion? Load of rubbish.'

One can, however, discern two elements in Judaism which influenced Regardie. The first is the notion of a code of honour. Unless one becomes a student of Kabbala, Judaism is not a metaphysical religion and one finds little concern with the afterlife: its concerns are ethical, involving how we act here and now. 'Honourable' is perhaps the highest word of praise a Jew uses for a particular action he or she respects. Throughout his life, Regardie endeavoured to be honourable.

The second notion is that of the Rabbi. In contrast to Roman Catholicism, for instance, the Rabbi has in Judaism no innate or divine superiority to other men and women. Rabbi means merely 'wise man', and traditionally the Rabbi has been simply the most learned man of any given Jewish community. He is expected to be married and to have children, not only for the sake of the Biblical commandment to Adam and Eve (and later to Abraham) to be fruitful and multiply, but also because of the practical, common-sensical belief that a man without a wife and children is perfectly useless and incapable of advising the community regarding marital and parental problems.

Nevertheless, and in common with so many Jews, Regardie came as a teenager to reject a religion which seemed to him to offer little more than a fierce, jealous and bloodthirsty father-figure roaring: 'Don't argue! Do as I say!' He also rejected the classic Jewish view of socio-economic personal development.

This is an issue which has been severely misunderstood. Even well-intentioned, decent people who abhor anti-semitism nevertheless appear to believe that the principal concern of the Jews is the making of money. This matter is somewhat less simplistic than it initially appears to be.

When the Jews were scattered, they had no position, money, security or status in the various societies into which they entered. There is one plain, clear way forward to a better life in any society at any time for any individual – the acquisition of money. This fact may well be deplorable but non-Jews who disrespect money are hard to find. Harder to find, in fact, than Jews like Freud, Marx or Einstein, who laboured all their lives for the advancement of humanity with a pittance as their reward.

In the Middle Ages the Roman Catholic Church (which until recently blamed the crucifixion of Christ upon the Jews) recognized the essential importance of money-lending to trade, yet condemned the practice as usury. Christians were therefore forbidden to lend money at interest – yet this was essential to the flourishing of commerce. Therefore the despised Jews were licensed to practise usury and condemned on account of it. A poor, down-trodden and persecuted people saw an opportunity to improve their unenviable lot and seized it. For generation after generation Jews acquired expertise as bankers and merchants. Their position in society was based upon money.

Yet despite this dependence upon financial skills forced upon the Jews by the society around them, they did not forget an earlier tradition, the tradition of learning. Anyone can see from the impassioned conviction of the Hebrew Prophets in the Old Testament, for instance, that it is better to be learned than loaded. The result, which evolved from the mating of worldly and divine wisdom, has become a cliché of Jewish-American comedy. 'Be a doctor, my son, be a lawyer . . .' which ingeniously combines learning, culture, social position and money. This is a Jewish ideal. Many fail to understand that, for example, a Jewish businessman who has been born in appalling poverty and who subsequently makes millions would prefer a son who became a cultured, well-educated barrister with a good though not spectacular income to one who continued as a vulgar tycoon.

It is necessary to probe and explore these sensitive areas, for we are trying to comprehend the factors which affected the man Regardie. He would return to this earlier conditioning in later life, though after another manner, when he would support his magical endeavours through earning a richly deserved living as a psychotherapist and in testy moods he would grumble: 'Why're Magicians usually so poor? You never meet a poor Christian Scientist.'

Moreover, throughout his life, he was sensitive about the matter of being Jewish. The reprehensible anti-semitic attitudes of too many English people during his times in Britain no doubt brought about this undesirable consequence. His attitude remained consistently ambivalent. For instance, in old age he was wont to criticize acidly certain Jewish attitudes while tucking in heartily to the excellent Jewish food he'd cooked. According to Laura Jennings, though this is not the account I originally received, Regardie died with his face in a bowl of chicken soup. If this is so, then there is surely something very Zen about his manner of departure.

However, his initial reaction to his upbringing was that of any healthy teenager: he rebelled against it. In place of law or medicine or anything else which would have pleased his father and mother, he chose art, that most insecure of professions and then – far worse in the eyes of Jewish parents – the occult. His first doorway was, as has been said, Theosophy.

This was appropriate. It has been said that the Jews are the bridge between East and West: and Theosophy served as a bridge to Eastern thought for many Westerners. At the time too, Theosophy served to introduce so many to the occult and to mind-expansion.

What can sensibly be said about Madame Blavatsky's extraordinary works? One reads them and is confronted by ideas and assertions which flatly contradict anything one might read in the papers or hear at home or learn at school. These assertions, supported by astounding data, are piled on so thick and fast that any sane brain is sent reeling after due open-minded contemplation.

Suppose that you have an immortal spirit within you, which has been on earth so very many times before in one body or another and which will go, not to heaven or to hell, but to a hundred, a thousand or even many million more lives. Suppose that karma is indeed a law of the Universe, that everything you do will inevitably come back to you sooner or later. Suppose that there are indeed Hidden Masters, beings of praeter-human intelligence, who are concerned with the evolution of life upon this planet and who may get in touch with you if they think you have potential and may be useful. Suppose that there are practices by which you can expand your awareness, enhance your every faculty, come into contact with non-physical beings of various kinds, transform your life and lift yourself to states of consciousness whereby, if you yourself are not a Hidden Master, you are at least in their class . . . one may indeed disagree totally with these notions, so trenchantly advanced by Madame Blavatsky, but it cannot be denied that even a momentary acceptance will vastly expand the horizons of the mind.

Furthermore, belief in these suppositions – rightly or wrongly – can transform one's whole life. That may or may not be desirable, and obviously one judges by results, but it is hard to see what Regardie could lose by his enthusiastic adolescent embracing of these ideas. It is certainly true that this makes one's time more lively and interesting.

That is what happened to the young Regardie. And the point which attracted his finest attention was practical. Madame Blavatsky had declared that many things of which she wrote were comprehensible only to 'Adepts'. Very well: if this is so, how does one become an Adept? How can these propositions be tested in the light of experience? If one is open-minded, it is surely a matter of finding a set of time-honoured practices alleged to bring one to the states desired and of working at them for a reasonable period of time.

Regardie set out to do this while still in his mid-teens and, fortunately, a time-honoured method, sanctioned by Madame Blavatsky, was available.

Yoga.

Notes

1 *The Voice of The Silence*, with a superb commentary by 'Frater O.M.' (Aleister Crowley) has been published in *The Equinox*, Vol. III, No. 1, also known as *The Blue Equinox*, a publication edited and largely written by Crowley; and in *Gems From The Equinox*, edited by Regardie.

2 For the record, the author takes pride in the fact that his father's family is Jewish, although this entails the unfortunate consequence that he would have been gassed in Nazi Germany, yet is not accepted as Jewish by the state of Israel.

2

Yoga and the Intelligent Teenager

Regardie's quest for meaning and purpose in life was spurred onward by the experience of emotions common to so many intelligent and sensitive adolescents. One of these experiences is of especial relevance here. Its nature and quality and importance to Western Man have been explored brilliantly, for instance, by Colin Wilson in *The Outsider*. The Outsider is one 'who sees too deep and too much' as a result of which he becomes alienated from the herd and its material concerns, for he is appalled by the futility of all human endeavour. Buddhists call this the Trance of Sorrow. Others might term it 'an existential crisis'. All who have experienced it agree on three points: the feeling is one of bitter agony; eventually they become conscious of a ravenous hunger and infinite yearning, suspected in themselves to be futile, for some secret glory which will restore some essential meaning to life; and it changes their fundamental point of view for a lifetime.

Impelled by a hunger for wisdom beyond the material, for a life that was something more than merely 'birth, copulation and death', to use Eliot's phrase, Regardie studied Eastern philosophy and Yoga and was familiar with the major works by the time he was eighteen. Although he was not yet familiar with the works of Aleister Crowley, Regardie's intellectual position can be succinctly summarized in the words of the former:

> We perceive in the sensible world, Sorrow. Ultimately that is: We admit the existence of a Problem requiring solution. . . . Following on this we say: If any resolution there be to . . . the Vanity of Life and the Vanity of Thought, it must be in the attainment of a Consciousness which transcends both of them. Let us call this supernormal

consciousness, or, for want of a better name 'Spiritual Experience' (*The Equinox*, I, 2).

This is surely straightforward enough – yet so much rubbish has been written and spoken about Yoga. So much advantage has been and still is taken of Western ignorance. The West has to endure a plethora of 'Holy Men' whom the East would regard as clowns. There are 'teachers' who have precious little to teach; books from which nothing useful can be learned; classes which give the gullible fatuous fibs as a substitute for truth. And the test of truth with Yoga is really terribly simple. It is the same as the test of truth in any other sphere of human knowledge. It is: are the facts correct? and how can this be tested? and is the logic coherent? Any statement which does not pass these elementary tests is no part of Yoga.

As Aleister Crowley stated, 'Yoga' comes from the same etymological root as the Latin *jugum* – a yoke – and it means 'union'. Yoga yokes together the perceiver and the thing perceived, the knower and the thing known – and leads to a union between the two. Yogis declare that the experience of this union is so powerful that it transforms one's life.

However, the teenage Regardie was not yet prepared for practices. First he studied the philosophical context of the subject, reading Hindu classics such as *The Upanishads* and *The Bhagavad-Gita*, which he would always revere, in addition to other scriptures and manuals of instruction. He came to realize that Hinduism is a synthesis of the various cults of the Indian sub-continent. A Hindu can believe in any god, goddess or gods and/or goddesses whatsoever as long as there is commitment to the caste system. The caste system is a way of ordering social life. It is thought by Hindus that there are four classes of society: in descending order, these are the priestly caste, (Brahmins); the warrior caste; the merchant caste; and the worker caste; below these, there are the 'Untouchables'.

In common with any sensible Westerner, Regardie had little interest in the Hindu caste system but he perceived that Theosophy derived from the religion. Why are Hindus so tolerant in matters of religious thought? The answer is in that noble document of the human spirit, *The Upanishads*, and the sages who created the system of thought we know as Vedanta. This was an attempt to make order out of the chaos of the innumerable Indian cults. Vedanta is the supreme expression of the Hindu religion and, paradoxically, it also justifies the superstitious behaviour of the peasants.

The ultimate reality is called Brahman. Brahman is the utterly impersonal force out of which the Universe derives its manifestation. Brahman is neither male nor female. It is beyond manifestation; it is the ultimate reality.

Everything that is not Brahman is Maya, or illusion. In other words, the manifested Universe is an illusion. We, as imperfect beings, have to deal with this illusion. There is something within us which knows it is an illusion. This something is called '*atman*' - the ultimate spirit or soul - and it is part of Brahman. It is, if one chooses to express it in this way, God within us. We undertake incarnation after incarnation until we realize this, and according to Vedanta, our aim must be to become one with our *atman* and so part of Brahman, liberated eternally from Maya. That, it is declared, is our object of existing.

The attentive reader will no doubt have spotted an obvious objection here. What is the point of not being one with Brahman and so existing in Maya or Illusion, solely in order to become, in the end, one with Brahman? The answer is best left to Hindu theologians. The purpose here is simply to expound and explain the viewpoint of Vedanta insofar as it can be done.

It is believed that nearly all sentient beings are not one with Brahman and so exist in the world of Maya. How, if at all, does Brahman manifest here? This is where the gods come in. It is held that the Energy of Brahman manifests in the forces and forms of gods - and goddesses. The initial manifestation in a Universe of illusion is normally portrayed as a trinity of gods - Brahma the Creator; Vishnu the Preserver; and Shiva the Destroyer. These three Powers have goddesses with whom they consort and they manifest more densely as other gods and goddesses. These in turn manifest yet more densely and on every level of human life, the result being roughly three hundred and twenty million deities, all of whom are part of Brahma, Vishnu or Shiva, and hence part of Brahman. Thus, when a peasant chooses to worship the divinity of his fire-place, responsible to the divinity of his village, he is worshipping an aspect of Brahman and thus making contact with It.

In addition, there is the doctrine of *avatars*. This means that a god or goddess comes to Earth in a human body. The most famous example of this is Krishna, an *avatar* of Vishnu the Preserver, but there are many others. Thus it would be perfectly possible to revere Jesus Christ as an avatar of God while remaining a pious Hindu.

There is the belief in *karma* – the Law of Cause and Effect, whereby everything you do will come back to you. This belief is often misunderstood. I have heard it seriously argued, for instance, that if I eat too much poached salmon, I will have to reincarnate as a salmon and be eaten by the salmon reincarnated as a human being – when in fact the consequence of my action is likely to be indigestion. Finally, there is the belief in reincarnation. It is held that the *atman* migrates from body to body over the ages. We die only to be reborn in a future life. The ultimate aim of this is, as I have stated, to attain *Moksha* or liberation from the wheel of birth, death and rebirth, whereby we become one with Brahman. And one may well ask: what is the point of Brahman putting out points, each of which is *atman*, to enter Illusion onlyto come back again? – but again, let us leave this to Hindu theologians.

Any student of Western philosophy must have noticed similarities between Vedanta and the thought of Bishop Berkeley. For Berkeley argued that the world of matter is illusory; that things exist only by virtue of being perceived; and that if we didn't perceive them, they wouldn't exist at all, were it not for God – or Brahman – who is always everywhere and perceiving everything.

Unsurprisingly, Regardie's study of Hinduism extended to Buddhism and the reading of classics like *The Dhammapada* and *The Questions of King Milinda*. Buddhism is the most logically coherent of all the organized religions. It holds that there was a man called Gautama who was born a Hindu prince. Although his parents did all they could to shield him from the pains of life on earth, he once saw a beggar and this made him so desperately unhappy that he fled his palace in search of enlightenment. Finally, or so it is said, he found it. It is related that after many adventures, Gautama sat beneath the sacred bodhi tree for forty days and forty nights, refusing to move until he had attained enlightenment. Having achieved this, he was called 'Buddha' by his followers – 'Buddha' means 'Enlightened One'. He then proclaimed the Four Noble Truths: (a) Existence is Suffering – a realization which so often spurs adolescents – and adults – onto a quest for wisdom; (b) the cause of Suffering is Craving; (c) the cessation of Suffering therefore means the cessation of Craving; and (d) the way to achieve that is to follow what Gautama Buddha called 'The Noble Eight-Fold Path'. This consists of eight principles of conduct and mental training.

In addition, Buddha denied a number of beliefs which Hindus hold sacred. He thought that the caste system was utterly ridiculous. Many Westerners would agree; but Gautama went much further. As the Buddhist proverb has it:

Birth is Misery.
Life is Misery.
Death is Misery.
But Resurrection is the greatest Misery of all.

With complete consistency of logic, Buddha proceeded to deny both Brahman and *atman*. In other words, he denied that there is a One behind the Universe and he denied that there is within us a central spirit or soul. Whereas in Hinduism, this spirit or soul goes from body to body throughout countless incarnations until it finally becomes One with Brahman, in Buddhism there is no soul and there is no One. This is hard to grasp at first – but it is rather like looking at waves on a sea-shore. A wave comes and breaks, it withdraws, then another wave comes, which may contain much of the same water as before – and then it withdraws and another wave comes . . . there is no permanent 'central water' in these succeeding waves.

Again, the attentive reader may have noticed a significant parallel in Western philosophy – Hume. His thought is strikingly similar. In *A Treatise of Human Nature* and *An Enquiry Concerning Human Understanding*, Hume ridiculed the notion of there being a central 'Self' and regarded beliefs as being simply tendencies of the mind which did not stand up to rational analysis, a position similar to, if not identical with, Buddhist thought. Credit for discerning the similarities and identities between Vedantist thought and Berkeley, and Buddhist thought and Hume, has to go to Aleister Crowley, and it is astonishing that this matter is not studied in British universities.

There are two major forms of Buddhism. The 'Mahayana' or 'Greater Vehicle' is to be found mainly in India, China, Japan, Tibet and Nepal. It has blended with the beliefs of the peoples it has influenced. As a result, we find in it the idea that there are many Buddhas or 'Enlightened Ones' and we can pray to them to give us better lives and better future incarnations – a hypothesis which Gautama, judging from the records, would have found preposterous. In India, it is hard to distinguish between Hindu and Mahayana Buddhist theory and practice. Nevertheless, the influence of Mahayana has been productive in its mating with certain beliefs held before its arrival: results have included a union with Bon so as to produce Tibetan Tantra; and a union with Chinese Tao-ist thought so as to produce Cha'an, which in Japan became Zen.

The earlier form of Buddhism, which is closest to the teaching of Gautama and his immediate disciples, is known as the 'Hinayana' or 'Lesser Vehicle' and as 'Theravada'. It is to be found mainly in South-east Asia, most notably Burma and Sri Lanka.

To turn our attention from theory to practice, there are very few books on the practice of Yoga which are worth reading.

This is a pity, for Yoga is the Way for Buddhists, whether Mahayana or Hinayana, and for Hindus. The goal of the Hindu is to have union with Brahman – Yoga means union. The goal of the Buddhist is Nirvana, that cessation of Existence which is Suffering, and so the ego must annihilate itself in that union with Nirvana (Nothingness) which is Yoga. Either way, the goal is union with Beyond Infinity. The essence of the matter is simplicity itself. As Crowley put it: 'Sit still. Stop thinking. Shut up. Get out.'

No more is actually needed for the practice of Yoga, but many may require more specific directions. Most texts will confuse more than they clarify. The texts written by semi-literate Hindus in the hope of making money and disciples out of gullible Westerners are the worst. The best are certain classics which Regardie studied: the *Yoga Aphorisms* of Patanjali; *Raja Yoga* by Swami Vivekananda, the great disciple of Ramakrishna; the *Shiva Sanhita*; the *Hathayoga Pradipika*; and the writings of 'Arthur Avalon' (Sir John Woodruffe). To these the present writer would add Theos Bernard's *Hatha Yoga* and a very good little book published by Pelican and called simply *Yoga* by Ernest Wood. Finally, perhaps beyond all these, there are the relevant works of Aleister Crowley.

Regardie first came across Crowley's name at the age of eighteen at the house of lawyer friend in Washington, DC. A work by this man was read aloud. It was called Part 1 of *Book Four*. Although Regardie was familiar with the classics, he was dazzled by Crowley's brilliance and clarity, and over forty years later, he would still insist in print that Part 1 of *Book Four* is a classic in its own right. The essentials of Raja Yoga – 'Royal Yoga', the Way of one-pointed concentration upon an object, real or imagined – are explored quietly, calmly and methodically; technical terms are avoided or else carefully explained; and it is obvious that the author is an experienced and accomplished Yogi. The essence of the matter is stated succinctly in the *Summary*:

Firstly, we still the body by the practice called Asana, and secure its ease and the regularity of its functions by Pranayama (breath-control). Thus no messages from the body will disturb the mind.

Secondly, by Yama and Niyama, we still the emotions and passions, and thus prevent them arising to disturb the mind.

Thirdly, by Pratyahara we analyse the mind yet more deeply, and begin to control and suppress thought in general of whatever nature.

Fourthly, we suppress all other thoughts by a direct concentration upon a single thought. This process, which leads to the highest results, consists of three parts, Dharana, Dhyana, and Samadhi, grouped under a single term Samyama.

Dharana is concentration, The process of Dhyana is described in *Book Four* as follows:

In the course of our concentration *we noticed that the contents of the mind at any moment consisted of two things, and no more*: the Object, variable, and the Subject, invariable, or apparently so. *By success in Dharana the object has been made as invariable as the subject ...*

Now the result of this is that the two become one. This phenomenon usually comes as a tremendous shock. It is indescribable even by the masters of language; and it is therefore not surprising that semi-educated stutterers wallow in oceans of gush.

All the poetic faculties and all the emotional faculties are thrown into a sort of ecstasy by an occurrence which overthrows the mind, and makes the rest of life seem absolutely worthless in comparison.

Samadhi, which Crowley attained, is beyond this. And so it is hardly surprising that a wildly enthusiastic Regardie wrote to Crowley care of the publisher. Eight months passed. Then, just when Regardie had forgotten his letter, a reply came from Paris. Crowley suggested that Regardie should contact his agent in New York, one Karl J. Germer. Regardie travelled to New York and discovered that Germer, an ex-Wehrmacht officer, was a passionate and sincere disciple of Crowley. From Germer, Regardie purchased ten bulky numbers of Crowley's *The Equinox*, a periodical published in London, 1909–14. The next stage of his quest would be an exploration of Magic – or, as Crowley called it, Magick.

3

The Approach to Magic

It is most unfortunate that the general public is so ill-informed on all matters relating to Ceremonial Magic and so it is perhaps best to begin by stating what it is not.

It is not about naked perverts prancing around a blood-stained altar upon which writhes a nude virgin over whom an unfrocked Roman Catholic priest mumbles Mass backwards while poncing about in semen-stained robes.

It is not about seedy suburbanites performing silly ceremonies so as to perk up their dreary little lives.

It is not about self-styled gurus, who would bore any sane person to the verge of insanity, imposing upon the impressionable with a preposterous pretence regarding secret information sources and claiming an omniscience ludicrous to all save the gullible.

It is not about a hoodoo-voodoo, mumbo-jumbo hotch-potch of bizarre terms repugnant to human intelligence. Nor is it about a merciful escape into a dream-world for the weak and wimpish; though it has to be regretfully admitted that the above five activities have all too frequently been carried on under the name of Magic.

Then what *is* Magic? Aleister Crowley defined it as 'the science and art of causing change to occur in conformity with will'. A later magician, Dion Fortune, limited the above by her definition: 'The science and art of causing changes in consciousness to occur in conformity with will,' though many practitioners of Magic would be comfortable with her point of view. The present writer has been known to define it as: 'The science and art of realising the Divine Self by changing the human self.'

What, then, is Black Magic? This over-used term is unfortunate. One cannot be comfortable with the racist connotations of the terminology. Moreover, we do not speak of black and white art or black and white science – so why black and white magic? One answer might be to point out that Magic is like water: one can use it to drive a hydro-electric power plant, make a cup of tea or boil one's granny; and that therefore Black Magic consists of the use of energies aroused through the practice of Magic to harm other individuals. Another point of view is that enunciated by Crowley in his *Magick: In Theory and Practice*:

> the single Supreme Ritual is the attainment of the Knowledge and Conversation of the Holy Guardian Angel. *It is the raising of the complete man in a vertical straight line.*
>
> ANY DEVIATION FROM THIS LINE TENDS TO BECOME BLACK MAGIC. ANY OTHER OPERATION IS BLACK MAGIC.

We shall be further inspecting these remarks; for the present it is important that terms used far too loosely in most cases are clearly defined.

Sorcery is the use of energies aroused through Magic for purely practical, material gain.

Witchcraft, as largely practised nowadays, is a religion claiming pagan ancestry which worships the male and female principles of Nature and uses sorcery to benefit those involved in that worship.

'Satanism' is a word which cannot be defined in one sentence, owing to the hysteria it arouses, but which denotes one or other of the following: (a) Perverted Christians who find it deliciously naughty to blaspheme their own religion; these seedy, overgrown schoolboys take puerile nonsense seriously. Many experienced prostitutes augment their incomes catering to their needs. (b) Wealthy degenerates who want salt with their sex and pepper with their perversions but who at least don't take the accompanying mummery seriously. (c) Jaded morons in search of some new kick, who've read some Dennis Wheatley novels or *Star* articles and have seen some horror films and who then vandalize churches or torture animals while bleating about the Devil. (d) Self-styled gurus whose magical practices have brought them a limited charisma and whose egotism is fed by the lost and inadequate whom they persuade to participate in black magic. (e) Anton Szandor LaVey's San Francisco-based Church of Satan, which equates 'Satan' with Freud's 'libido', uses ritualistic psycho-drama to liberate complexes, preaches ethics of enlightened self-interest and (predictably) attracts perfectly respectable yaps and yuppies. It should be clear from the foregoing that serious Magicians do not indulge in 'satanism' or 'Devil-worship.'

What leads people to the practice of Magic? Usually it is as a result of the quest for meaning and purpose in life, which has already been mentioned. If there is no meaning and purpose, it follows that it makes no difference whether you try to help humanity, shop for groceries or squirt sulphuric acid at maladjusted children: but if life does have a meaning and purpose, then one should endeavour to discover what it is.

Many have tried and a few have discovered truths which have created new civilizations – for example, Lao Tzu, Zoroaster, Gautama Buddha, Moses, Jesus called the Christ, or Mohammed. Others have contributed in less spectacular but nevertheless important ways. These truths have been discovered by a series of practices which alter consciousness and use largely untapped regions of the human brain. Nearly all teachers of these methods insist on solitude, certain rules of health and something usually called 'meditation' or 'prayer', which is the restraining of the mind to a single word, image or thought.

The brain, which gave Man dominion over the planet, is the hope for the human race; otherwise stupidity will lead inevitably to extinction. A very small portion of the brain is used by most people. Fortunately, there exist methods of tapping its vast resources.

Though these methods could be called simply ways of increasing human intelligence and potential, they are usually done within the context of a belief system and the goal is given a variety of names: for instance, samadhi, satori, enlightenment, liberation, even the Knowledge and Conversation of the Holy Guardian Angel. Some of the methods used have recently acquired intellectual respectability in the West: Yoga, Zen, Sufism, Buddhist meditation - how curious that Magic, which does the same thing, is often so misunderstood and despised, even though it is the most Western of Ways.

The method of Magic is to attain a total one-pointed concentration on a desired objective by using the natural tendency of the Western mind to turn outward - Yoga has the same objective, but here the mind turns inward. Magic might be termed the Yoga of the West. The wand, cup, sword, disk, incense, robes and geometric designs use this natural tendency to be stimulated by sights, sounds, scents, dramatic gesture and emotional exaltation so as to focus the will into a blazing stream of pure energy wholly concentrated upon one idea only.

Magicians have basic PT: exercises to improve relaxation, breathing, visualization and concentration. They use divination - whether by astrology, geomancy, I-Ching or Tarot - to develop intuition and perception. The exercise commonly known as 'astral travel' or 'scrying in the spirit vision' familiarizes the practitioner with other states and orders of being: or, according to another school of thought (for magicians aren't dogmatic), the contents of what Jung termed 'the Collective Unconscious'.

Evocation, or the calling forth of spirits, can be regarded as just that. Or one could see it as a drastic psychoanalytical process, whereby the spirit is a 'complex' and hence trapped energy. What the Magician is doing, therefore, is releasing trapped energy, hallucinating it as a personification and reintegrating it into his psyche. Or finally, one could say that he (or she) is exploring mysterious regions of the brain in order to activate hitherto unused cells.

Invocation, or the bringing down of gods and goddesses, can be regarded in at least two ways. Either there are certain invisible but powerful forces of Nature in the Universe, the existence of which is unsuspected by physical science, and which can inspire us with beauty and truth. Or there are certain archetypes of the Collective Unconscious latent in all of us which, when rightly stimulated, can inspire us with beauty and truth.

These practices of the Magician are done within a schema of progress, usually based upon the Tree of Life of the Kabbalists. The purpose of this model is not to mystify but to clarify and classify supra-rational states of being. It can be regarded as being, among other things, a map of consciousness and its various states.

Magic was known, studied and practised all over the Mediterranean basin before and during the time of the Roman Empire. The most unfortunate consequence of the Roman Empire's decline and fall was a relapse by the West into barbarism. Fortunately the civilization of Islam eventually arose and the wick of wisdom not only burned but blazed, and spread into Spain.

That admirable scholar, the late Dame Frances Yates, attributes the origins of Renaissance hermetic philosophy to the work of Ramon Lull of Moorish Spain. The writings of Lull give full credit to his teachers, the Sufis. And according to Yates and other scholars, this wisdom spread to Renaissance figures such as Cornelius Agrippa, Paracelsus and John Dee. This 'Renaissance Hermetic or Occult Philosophy' can be summarized in the following nine propositions.

1 All is a Unity, created and sustained by God through His Laws.
2 These Laws are predicated upon Number.
3 There is an art of combining Hebrew letters and equating them with Number so as to perceive profound truths concerning the nature of God and His dealings with Man.
4 Man is of divine origin. Far from being created out of dust, as in the *Genesis* account, he is in essence a star daemon.
5 As such, he has come from God and must return to Him.
6 It is essential to regenerate the divine essence within Man, and this can be done by the powers of his divine intellect.
7 According to the Kabbala, God manifests by means of ten progressively more dense emanations; and Man, by dedicating his

mind to the study of divine wisdom and by refining his whole being and by eventual communion with the angels themselves, may at last enter into the presence of God.

8 An accurate understanding of natural processes, visible and invisible, enables Man to manipulate these processes through the power of his will, intellect and imagination.

9 The Universe is an ordered pattern of correspondences: or as John Dee put it, 'Whatever is in the Universe possesses order, agreement and similar form with something else'.

The present writer concurs with the view of Yates that this 'occult philosophy' was the essence of Renaissance thought and later powered the abortive 'Rosicrucian Movement'. To confine the matter to England, it subsequently filtered through a variety of individuals and organizations – for example, Robert Fludd, Elias Ashmole and certain Freemasons – but by the beginning of the nineteenth century, the Scientific Revolution, so essential to human evolution and to which the Renaissance magi had contributed so nobly, had repudiated its ancestors; and its proponents sneered at the wisdom which had originally inspired its thrust. It was seriously said – and still is said by those ignorant of quantum physics – that if it cannot be measured, it does not exist. Nevertheless, this tradition of wisdom, now ill-dignified by the buzz word 'cranky', somehow continued.

During the nineteenth century, the magical tradition passed through the hands of Francis Barrett, Frederick Hockley, Kenneth MacKenzie and Sir Edward Bulwer-Lytton: and was influenced by the work of Eliphas Levi in France and the foundation in 1875 of Madame Blavatsky's Theosophical Society. Various threads were then knitted together in the Hermetic Order of the Golden Dawn, founded in 1887. The creator and synthesizer of the Golden Dawn system was Samuel Liddell 'MacGregor' Mathers. It was Mathers who welded together Renaissance occult philosophy, including and especially the Kabbala, with certain of its sources which had come to light by his own time – and his own inspiration. The result was a body of knowledge and a method for taking practical advantage of that knowledge. The entire system, the first nine volumes of which fill 870 pages in the latest edition, *The Complete Golden Dawn System of Magic* (1984), was then summarized and synthesized again in more concentrated form – 160 pages – within a refined paradigm deriving directly from the sixteenth-century 'angel-magic' of John Dee and Edward Kelly. The 'Adepts', who had mastered all the earlier knowledge and praxis, consequently found themselves confronted by a new learning which incorporated and surpassed the old; providing the aspirant with new maps for the exploration of other dimensions of existence, methods for so doing, and a language for communication with beings thereby encountered. In spite of schism and much undignified squabbling, and wholly unknown to the young Regardie, various groups deriving from the Golden Dawn were still pursuing their work in 1926. One could learn Order teaching only through meeting an initiate who would agree to introduce one to the Order, or through reading what Aleister Crowley had published in *The Equinox*.

Crowley's membership of the Golden Dawn, his departure from its Temple, various quarrels and the history of the Order itself will be explored in due course. It suffices to say that by 1909, when he commenced the publication of *The Equinox*, he had become a Master of Magick – he spelled the word with the Anglo-Saxon 'k' – and of Yoga in addition to the Adeptus Minor grade of initiation which had been conferred upon him by Mathers back in 1900. He had his own Order, the A∴A∴. Its existence was announced to the public with the slogan: 'The Method of Science. The Aim of Religion'; and it was announced in *The Equinox*. As Crowley wrote in his autobiography, *The Confessions*:

> *The Equinox* was the first serious attempt to put before the public the facts of occult science ... From the moment of its appearance, it imposed its standards of sincerity, scholarship, scientific seriousness and aristocracy of all kinds, from the excellence of its English to the

perfection of its printing, upon everyone with ambition to enter this field of literature ... It is recognised as the standard publication of its kind, as an encyclopedia without 'equal, son, or companion.' It has been quoted, copied and imitated everywhere.

In its pages, Regardie found further evidence of Crowley's proficiency at Yoga, especially demonstrated by the latter's beautifully clear manuals of practical instruction. *Liber E vel Exercitiorum* teaches physical clairvoyance, Asana (posture), Pranayama (regularization of the breathing) and Dharana (control of thought), together with a method of investigating one's physical limitations and a recommended course of reading in a mere seven pages. *Liber RV vel Spiritus* gives detailed teaching in Pranayama in four and a half pages. Nor are Crowley's prescriptions confined solely to the Way of Raja Yoga. *Liber CMXIII*, also called *Liber Thisharb*, gives instruction in Gnana Yoga, the Yoga of knowledge, which consists of training the intellect. *Liber Astarte* is probably the finest document extant on Bhakta-Yoga, the Yoga of uniting oneself to a particular deity by love and devotion. Tantric and Kundalini Yoga, which employ sexual energy, are dealt with too in manuals for advanced students. *Liber HHH* gives three methods of attainment through complex meditations, and its third method, *SSS*, is specifically concerned with the Kundalini, the Serpent Power at the base of the spine, which rises when correctly activated to unite with centres of energy within the brain and confers Enlightenment: and *Liber Yod* gives alternative ways of accomplishing the same objective.

Regardie's colossal admiration for Crowley's writings on Yoga, a subject with which he was familiar, spurred him on to eager study of Magic, with which he was not. He learned that the ceremonial Magician uses a variety of techniques to purify and exalt his body, imagination, sexuality, intellect, emotions, perception and moral character so that he is at last fitted to give his personality to a deeper individuality. This is also called the obtaining of the Knowledge and Conversation of the Holy

Guardian Angel. Once this is done, one knows one's true work in the world.

But it doesn't end there. This is the stage called Adeptship. The next task is to perfect the faculties of this deeper individuality – and then sacrifice it in a mystic marriage with the Universe itself. (Unfortunately, it is exceptionally difficult to avoid romantic language; or to communicate in words what is beyond them, as all mystics agree.) This stage – called the Crossing of the Abyss – annihilates the ego: 'the dew-drop slips into the shining sea', to use Arnold's phrase; and there arises a Master, one who has attained to Understanding.

A Master of Magic is in accord with a Master of Zen, or Yoga, or Sufism, for all true Ways are ultimately identical. But Magicians argue that Magic, which grew up in the West, is therefore better suited to the Western Mind than Eastern Ways. They are aware too that just as the Sufis, for instance, have been vilified by orthodox Muslims and only now are beginning once again to receive their just recognition, so Magic has been vilified by the enemies of Light and Truth.

Much of the Magician's work is done in solitude. In Part II of *Book Four*, the first part of which had so enthused Regardie, Crowley succinctly describes the tools of the ceremonial magus:

The Magician works in a *Temple*; the Universe, which is (be it remembered!) conterminous with himself. In this temple a *Circle* is drawn upon the floor for the limitation of his working. This circle is protected by divine names, the influences on which he relies to keep out hostile thoughts. Within the circle stands an *Altar* the solid basis on which he works, the foundation of all. Upon the Altar are his *Wand, Cup, Sword* and *Pantacle*, to represent his Will, his Understanding, his Reason, and the lower parts of his being, respectively. On the Altar, too, is a phial of *Oil*, surrounded by a *Scourge*, a *Dagger*, and a *Chain*, while above the Altar hangs a *Lamp*. The Magician wears a *Crown*, a single *Robe*, and a *Lamen*, and he bears a *Book* of Conjurations and a *Bell*.

The oil consecrates everything that is touched with it; it is his aspiration; all acts performed in accordance with that are holy. The scourge tortures him; the dagger wounds him; the chain binds him. It is by virtue of these three that his aspiration remains pure, and is able to consecrate all other things ... He wears a crown to affirm his lordship, his divinity; a robe to symbolise silence, and a lamen to declare his work. The book of spells or conjurations is his magical record, his Karma. In the East is the *Magic Fire*, in which all burns up at last.

The essential practices of the Magician – divination, evocation and invocation – have been described earlier. Of these, by far the most important is invocation, for this involves calling upon a god and thus the bringing of divine or super-consciousness into human consciousness. An example might make clearer the nature of magical work.

It is a vital part of the Magician's task to invoke and identify with all the gods and goddesses. Suppose, for example, that the god in question is Horus, Egyptian god of War, Force and Fire, the equivalent of the Roman Mars and the Greek Ares. The Magician will furnish his Temple – his laboratory or place of working – with corresponding symbols and things which suggest and reinforce the idea of Horus. These correspondences, which appear to reflect the structure of the tendencies of the Western mind, can be looked up in Crowley's *Seven Seven Seven* or later magical works of reference and derive from Golden Dawn teaching. The enquirer will find that the Number of Horus is five – and so employ at least one five-pointed star and five candles for illumination – the element is Fire, the plants sacred to Horus are Oak, Nux Vomica and Nettle, the precious stone sacred to the God is the Ruby, the appropriate weapon or magical instrument with which to gesture is the Sword, the incense is Tobacco and/or the substance known as Dragon's Blood, the metal is Iron and the colour is Red. The Magician procures some if not all of these and arranges the Temple with as much artistry as he can. The place of working and the accompanying paraphernalia must then be purified and consecrated.

There follow what are known as the Lesser Banishing

Rituals of the Pentagram and Hexagram, short rituals designed to prevent interference from any influence foreign to the purpose of the operation. The Magician then proceeds with the business of invocation, endeavouring ultimately to identify with the god, to become one with him. There are a number of tried and tested methods but much is left to the practitioner's own ingenium. Crowley states the essence of the matter in *Magick: In Theory and Practice*:

> The Magician addresses a direct petition to the Being invoked. But the secret of success in invocation has not hitherto been disclosed. It is an exceedingly simple one. It is of practically no importance whatever that the invocation should be 'right'. There are a thousand different ways of compassing the end proposed, so far as external things are concerned. The whole secret may be summarised in these four words: '*Enflame thyself in praying*'.
>
> The mind must be exalted until it loses consciousness of self. The Magician must be carried forward blindly by a force which, though in him and of him, is by no means that which he in his normal state of consciousness calls I. Just as the poet, the lover, the artist, is carried out of himself in creative frenzy, so must it be for the Magician . . .
>
> *Every Magician must compose his ceremony in such a manner as to produce a dramatic climax. At the moment when the excitement becomes ungovernable, when the whole conscious being of the Magician undergoes a spiritual spasm, at that moment must he utter the supreme adjuration . . .*
>
> *Inhibition is no longer possible or even thinkable, and the whole being of the Magician, no minutest atom saying nay, is irresistibly flung forth. In blinding light, amid the roar of ten thousand thunders, the Union of God and man is consummated.*

There is little point in debating whether the God thus invoked has objective or subjective existence. Seven words of Crowley's summarize the central point: 'By doing certain things, certain things happen.'

In his study of *The Equinox*, Regardie's appreciation of Crowley grew, for he found him to be the clearest and most authoritative writer on Ritual Magic. Although Regardie initially had to struggle with unfamiliar terms, he would express his lasting admiration fifty years later when he would edit that masterly selection of magical writings, *Gems From The Equinox*. The instructions for practical work are the simplest and most succinct. *Liber O vel Manus et Sagittae*, for instance, is only fifteen pages long, yet it gives instructions for elementary study of the Kabbala, Assumption of God forms, Vibration of Divine Names, the Rituals of the Pentagram and the Hexagram, and their use in protection and invocation, a method of attaining astral visions and an instruction in a practice called Rising on the Planes. A dedicated student could easily spend a year working on it; Regardie did. Moreover the preliminary remarks display a refreshing common sense:

> 2. In this book it is spoken of the Sephiroth, and the Paths, of Spirits and Conjurations; of Gods, Spheres, Planes and many other things which may or may not exist.
>
> It is immaterial whether they exist or not. By doing certain things certain results follow: students are most earnestly warned against attributing objective reality or philosophic validity to any of them.
>
> 3. The advantages to be gained from them are chiefly these:
>
> (a) A widening of the horizon of the mind.
>
> (b) An improvement of the control of the mind.

Crowley concentrated on the essentials of the Golden Dawn system and endeavoured to eliminate the inessentials. In the course of doing this, he perceived the disadvantages of group working, which include personality clashes, squabbles and schism; the difficulties a student may suffer in trying to link up with genuine magical Order; and the advantages of solitude. As a result of experiences and initiations undergone after he left the Golden Dawn, Crowley composed new rituals of striking beauty and power whereby a student working alone could accomplish effective Magic.

Regardie's encounter with Magic, as he put it, 'changed the course of my whole life'. He examined himself and 'I realised

I was no artist.' As Colin Wilson aptly remarks in his Introduction to Regardie's *Energy, Prayer and Relaxation*: 'Fate had marked him out for a rather more strange and interesting career.' He became good friends with Karl Germer, who served as liaison with Crowley. The result was that Crowley eventually offered Regardie a post as his secretary and invited the latter to join him in Paris. Although Crowley had recently received atrocious publicity both in the English and the American gutter press, Regardie seized this opportunity for adventure.

Unfortunately, there were complications. He was not yet twenty-one years old, and so was legally a minor. In order to obtain the necessary diplomatic instruments of travel – a passport from the US State Department and a visa from the French Consul in Washington DC – he had to present his father's written consent. Telling the latter that he would be staying with a man recently described as 'the wickedest man in the world' was clearly out of the question, so Regardie stated that he had been invited to study painting with an English artist in Paris. His father agreed to this and gave him the necessary document for the passport office.

When it was time to obtain the French visa, however, Regardie simply couldn't face going through the same bothersome procedure all over again. This time he typed a letter purporting to come from his father and forged his signature. All he needed now was the boat ticket. That was hardly a problem. And so, as Regardie put it in *The Eye In The Triangle*:

> On the night in October 1928 when I set sail from New York for Paris, there was a pleasant dinner at a good New York restaurant. Present were Karl Germer and Cora Eaton, who subsequently became his wife, Dorothy Olsen (a former mistress of Crowley), my sister and myself. Conviviality was the law that night. Everyone enjoyed himself with a good dinner and good wine and good conversation, except my sister who acted as a wet blanket. But on that occasion nothing could dampen my spirits; it was a celebration of my confrontation with destiny.

4

The Wickedest Man in the World

'Do what thou wilt shall be the whole of the law.'

It was with these words that Aleister Crowley, the Great Beast 666, greeted Israel Regardie at the Gare St Lazare, Paris. Regardie was understandably nervous. By his own account, he was timid, shy and introverted, a virgin who had led a somewhat studious, sheltered and retiring life, which factors made his venture all the more courageous.

These days, it is very hard indeed to understand the hysteria aroused then by the mere mention of Crowley's name. As late as the 1950s – a few years after Crowley's death, an ex-wife of an ex-disciple, called The Lady by John Symonds in *The Magic of Aleister Crowley* and Jean Overton Fuller in *The Magical Dilemma of Victor Neuberg*, would state her law for her guests: 'That name is never to be mentioned in this house.' It is difficult to find a contemporary parallel which would evoke the horror aroused in all respectable citizens by the contemplation of Regardie's action. It was looked upon, perhaps, as if one were going to see Ian Brady, or the Kray twins or Charles Manson for some advice. Tabloids such as *The Sunday Express* and *John Bull* had spent yards of newsprint over many years of assassinating Crowley's character. Here are some examples from *John Bull*.

THE KING OF DEPRAVITY (10 March 1923)
THE WICKEDEST MAN IN THE WORLD (24 March 1923)
KING OF DEPRAVITY ARRIVES (14 April 1923)
A CANNIBAL AT LARGE (April 1923)
A MAN WE'D LIKE TO HANG (May 1923)

To anyone idiotic enough to believe what is printed in publications devoid of quality and integrity, Regardie's action was the crassest folly with sinister aspects. Why, the poor, young, innocent boy was clearly offering himself as yet another helpless victim of Crowley's revolting, black magical, debauched and perverted blasphemy and might even be used as a human sacrifice before being cut up, cooked and eaten by the Beast. As for any alleged merit in Crowley's writings, hadn't that great arbiter of intellectual and aesthetic questions, the *Sunday Express*, settled the matter on 26 November 1922?

A large number of his books are printed privately – some of them in Paris. They are either incomprehensible or disgusting – generally both. His language is the language of a pervert and his ideas are negligible.

How could Regardie have been so naive? Or – possibly – so discerning?

The answer is distinctly to the credit of the shy youth who sailed from America with his life savings in his pocket. He had an independent mind which was practical and logical. Unlike too many, instead of rotting his brains with sensationalist nonsense, he read good books. A number of them were written by Crowley. Regardie could not honestly believe that the author of these good books, which had inspired him beyond anything he had ever known, given him clear instructions for the attainment of states of consciousness after which he sought so earnestly, and stimulated his mind to an unanticipated degree, could be the same man as the character of fiction whom the press kept calling a vile monster.

Fortunately, Regardie was right. The facts of the matter bear no relation to the ludicrous lies the most irresponsible papers printed. How did this extraordinary dichotomy between truth and falsehood arise? It is necessary to inspect this matter, for Crowley would have a dynamic, life-long effect on Regardie.

Aleister Crowley was born Edward Alexander Crowley on 12 October 1875 at Leamington Spa, Warwickshire. His father, Edward Crowley, was a wealthy, retired brewer.

His mother, Emily Bertha Bishop, came from a Devon and Somerset family. Both parents were Plymouth Brethren: that is to say they were members of the extreme Christian sect, founded by John Nelson Darby, which insists on the literal interpretation of the Bible as the exact words of the Holy Ghost. Crowley survived this upbringing and unsurprisingly, rebelled against it in his teens. After unhappy periods at various schools, including Malvern and Tonbridge, interspersed with periods of severe illness and education at the hands of private tutors, he went up to Trinity College, Cambridge in 1895. Although he thoroughly enjoyed his time there, he left in 1898 without taking a degree. He had inherited a sum of roughly £40,000, a fortune by the standards of the time, and was 'white-hot' on three pursuits: poetry, mountaineering and Magic.

His first published poem was *Acaldema* (1898) and, from that time on, poetry would pour from his pen so that during 1905–7 he would issue his *Collected Works* in three substantial volumes. As a mountaineer he undertook climbs on Beachy Head, the Lake District and the Alps which have never been repeated. As an aspiring Magician he joined the Golden Dawn in 1898 and speedily passed its examinations and climbed up its Grade system, assisted by intensive tuition from his great friend, the Adept Allan Bennett.

In 1900 a serious quarrel erupted between the Order Head, Mathers, then living in Paris, and his deputies in London. There were a number of issues: one was Crowley. The London chiefs strongly disapproved of the latter's reckless sex-life: by contrast, Mathers – who was married but celibate – insisted that a member's private life was entirely his or her own affair. The London chiefs refused to grant Crowley the intiation into Adeptship to which he was fully entitled and so the latter travelled to Paris, received it from Mathers and took his side in the quarrel, returning to London as his envoy. After a series of complex events beyond the scope of this work, Crowley decided that he was simply too inexperienced to cope with the legal and – he claimed – magical assaults of the London

Adepts, who included the poet, William Butler Yeats, and departed for Mexico.

There he achieved a series of world mountaineering records with his friend and partner, Oscar Eckenstein, and went on to Ceylon, where his mentor, Allan Bennett, was now domiciled. Here Crowley studied and practised Yoga, attaining the trance of Dhyana, before proceeding to rejoin Eckenstein for an abortive but record-setting attempt to climb K2, the world's second highest mountain. After further travels in India and Burma, he returned to his home in Scotland, 1903. There he married Rose Kelly, sister of Sir Gerald, later President of the Royal Academy. There was an extended honeymoon, involving travel through France, Italy, Egypt and India, before the couple returned to Egypt for the experience Crowley regarded as being the most important of his eventful life.

Rose, who had virtually no interest in Magic, asked Crowley to perform a minor ritual purely out of curiosity. Soon afterwards, she was possessed by a strange inspiration and declared to her husband that 'they are waiting for you', eventually informing him that 'they' meant in particular the God Horus. A sceptical Crowley carried out a series of tests based upon the traditional correspondences of the god and although Rose had no knowledge at all of occultism, she guessed correctly every time against total odds of 21,168,000 to 1. Some bewildering coincidences followed, all of which identified Crowley with The Beast 666 of Revelations. The upshot of all this was that Crowley performed an invocation to Horus and obeyed his wife's instructions to sit at a desk in his hotel room on 8, 9 and 10 April 1904 between 12 noon and 1 o'clock. A being which announced himself as Aiwass appeared behind him on each occasion and dictated to him the three chapters of a book called *Liber AL vel Legis* or *The Book of the Law*.

Judged on one level, *The Book of the Law* is an extraordinarily beautiful prose-poem but it declares itself to be much, much more. It proclaimed nothing less than that an Age had come to an end, that of Osiris, the God who died and rose again, known also as Adonis, Attis, Dionysus and Jesus Christ: and the age of Horus, the Crowned and Conquering Child of Isis and Oriris, had replaced it. Crowley was hailed as The Beast 666, Prophet of a New Aeon, in which the supreme commandment would be: *Do what thou wilt shall be the whole of the law.*

This does *not* mean anything as trite as 'Do whatever you want.' It means: find your True Will - whether it be the making of books or the making of tables, the farming of land or the running of industry, the way of the warrior or the way of the lover - and do that and nothing else. *Do what thou wilt* bids water to seek its level, sheep to eat grass and wolves to eat sheep. Yet surprisingly, Crowley wholly rejected the role which had been so unexpectedly thrust upon him and found *The Book of the Law* to be uncomfortable reading. Philosophically, he was then a Buddhist, and so could not accept its bald assertion that 'Existence is pure joy.' As a Romantic humanitarian, he was put off by its exaltation in the destruction of the Old Aeon. As a sceptic, he was embarrassed by its railing of him as The Beast 666, come to destroy the power of Christianity and liberate Mankind, for he regarded a belief in oneself as The Great Prophet as evidence of delusion and insanity. Within a short space of time, he lost the manuscript.

In 1905; Crowley led another abortive but record-setting mountaineering expedition, this time an attempt on Kangchenjunga, the world's third highest mountain. There followed a journey through Southern China and a series of intense mystical and magical experiences. Returning to London, he continued to write poetic and mystical literature, founded his magical Order, the A .·. A .·., and commenced publication of *The Equinox* in 1909. That was also the fateful year when he found the missing manuscript of *The Book of the Law* after five years of fighting against its acceptance: this time he embraced it whole-heartedly; it became the spine of his life. A series of extraordinary experiences undergone in the Sahara confirmed him in his belief, his conviction that as The Beast 666, it was his divinely appointed task to redeem humanity from what he termed 'the slave-gods' and bring about the New Aeon.

The next few years were difficult though productive. Crowley's marriage broke up, which caused him much personal agony, and his fortune was exhausted. The gutter press commenced its attacks upon him. Yet he managed to travel, write a number of extremely fine magical and poetical works – including *Book Four* – supervise his Order, become English-speaking Head of another magical Order, the Ordo Templi Orientis, investigate the effects of sex and drugs upon consciousness and love freely. From 1914 to 1919, he lived in the United States. It is alleged that he supported his magical endeavours by turning traitor during the First World War and writing pro-German propaganda: and also that he was in fact working for British Naval Intelligence. In the opinion of the present writer, the latter was the case; the evidence for this has been presented in my *Legacy of The Beast*; and certainly, Crowley was not prosecuted as a traitor on his return to England.

In 1920 The Beast founded his Abbey of Thelema at Cefalu, Sicily. This was soon the target of the gutter press and after some years of productive work, Crowley was finally expelled by order of Mussolini in 1923. From 1923 to 1928 Crowley divided his time between North Africa, notably Tunisia, Germany, where he had been elected World Head of the Ordo Templi Orientis, and Paris. When Regardie met Crowley, the latter was living in a comfortable apartment with 'Miroslava', his mistress.

All this sounds wholly laudable and innocent, almost tame. Then why did Crowley become the target of a campaign of vilification perhaps without parallel in English literary history? There are a number of reasons, or more correctly, since one is exploring a manifestation of hysteria, a number of causes. No one can whitewash Aleister Crowley, which is fortunate. Certainly he had his vices and he never veiled them in virtuous words. He was, among many other things, a Late Victorian bad boy. Today we would call him a Superbrat. He could be arrogant, disdainful and insulting. On the credit side, he always said exactly what he thought; an admirable practice which usually offends smug, self-righteous people. He liked sex very much and had no problem in attracting beautiful people to enjoy it with him, thus arousing the jealous fury of the repressed and incapable. He took drugs – so do so many and so what? – but this provoked morbid enmity among the neurotic. If someone accused him of cannibalism, for instance, and cited an alleged incident, he would calmly respond that the accusation was too mild and, with every appearance of sincerity, demand that 150 crimes of cannibalism per year for the years 1912–28 also be taken into consideration: and then would be wholly astounded to find his statements printed and believed.

Above all else, however, he advocated the evolution of human consciousness which, he argued, following *The Book of the Law*, begins with a recognition and acceptance of our reality as animals who should live according to the Law of Nature; after which, and only after which, we can progress to the Great Work of higher evolution. People who tell truths are usually lied about and persecuted and so was he.

What could Regardie learn from Cowley? Firstly, he hoped for personal tuition in Magic and to this end, Regardie had been working diligently at the appropriate practices, going so far as to use the tiny ship's cabin in which he had crossed the Atlantic as a magical temple. He hoped also for personal tuition in Yoga. He wanted to learn all he could from a Master he admired – yet, as is often the case with these matters, his time with Crowley was hardly as he had expected. He had reckoned without a variety of factors, including Crowley's remarkable ability to cause spiritual crises in people.

According to Regardie, this had nothing to do with Crowley's allegedly 'staring', 'hypnotic', 'mesmeric' or 'frightening' eyes: he found them simply 'small, warm, friendly and alive' and they 'gleamed pleasantly over the dark bags beneath them'. However, there were other aspects of Crowley which he found disconcerting.

When I arrived in Paris [Regardie told the present writer], I had about twelve hundred dollars on me, my entire life savings. Well, suddenly Crowley said: 'Got any money on you, Regardie?' and like the young fool I was, I handed it over and he went and spent it on champagne and brandy – always the best for him – and I never saw it again. Except in another sense. Later, when I was stuck in Brussels for months because I couldn't get entry back into England, it was the old man who supported me financially throughout that time, so it all worked out even. Then when I finally arrived in England, he had a few quid so he sent me to his tailor in Jermyn Street, as I recall. 'One needs a good suit in England, Regardie,' he said. 'Have one made and tell them to send me the bill.'

Regardie was a little disturbed by his first dinner with Crowley and Miroslava, who hailed from Poland. The excellent meal was served with the utmost style and ceremonial formalities – Regardie worried over which knife and fork to use for the various courses. Then, as the cognac came round: 'Crowley pounced on Miroslava and they fell down on the floor and started fucking like a pair of animals right there in front of me. Today that wouldn't bother me one jot, but then ... I was so amazed, I think I just staggered out of the room.'

One evening Miroslava had dinner with Regardie, told him she'd packed her bags and was leaving Crowley that very night and entrusted him with the unpleasant duty of telling Crowley the news. Crowley received it impassively then made his deadpan reply: 'The Lord hath given. The Lord hath taken away. Blessed be the Name of the Lord.' And that was that.

Crowley soon found a replacement in Maria Teresa de Miramar, a High Priestess of Voodoo from Nicaragua, whom Regardie described as 'a magnificent animal of a woman'. But as he later reminisced:

That pair used to have the most godawful rows, though. The trouble was that Crowley loved giving it to her up the arse and she used to get sick of it. When she was annoyed, she suddenly used to turn on him and hiss: '*Pederast!*' And he'd be going: 'Oh, *mon cherie*, how can you say this to me?' as he tried to kiss her and she'd still be hissing '*Pederast!*' until finally he grabbed her and they'd start fucking again.

One frequent and welcome visitor to this unlikely Parisian ménage was Gerald Yorke, then an impassioned disciple of Crowley. Yorke was an English country gentleman, educated at Eton and Cambridge, who'd once played first-class county cricket for Gloucestershire. According to Regardie:

> Yorke and I never had a great deal in common. There were only occasional distant-friendly chats. Our only bond of union was our common interest in Crowley, otherwise we would never have met. But I do recall, on one occasion when he let his hair down or I did, and we mutually confessed our latent apprehensions about the possibility of 'the old boy', as we familiarly called him, trying some homosexual monkey-tricks with either one. We were both relieved to find out that we shared this anxiety ... And we were even more relieved that nothing really had transpired.

Both Yorke and Regardie also marvelled at Crowley's mastery of chess. Crowley would play against both of them at once; they would sit with their boards before them; and Crowley would sit in an adjacent room, sipping cognac as he held an accurate picture of both boards in his mind – and go on to beat both of them.

Regardie's secretarial duties were not too onerous. Back in the United States and with his customary thoroughness, he had prepared himself by purchasing a Stenotype, a shorthand machine, and through practice acquired a workable speed of well over a hundred words per minute. Crowley's major preoccupation at that time was attending to the publication of a masterpiece, *Magick: In Theory and Practice*, and to the extensive correspondence he conducted, but early on he attended to a minor detail of Regardie's personal appearance. Crowley began by dictating a letter to an unnamed correspondent. Regardie dutifully took the letter down, typing more or less automatically. Then, as he later recalled in *The Eye in the Triangle*:

> towards the end of the letter, in the last paragraph, he added quite nonchalantly, something to the effect that you might consider examining your fingernails more closely. Other people do, and judge you accordingly. An occasional manicure might prove more than useful, etc., etc.
>
> In my stupidity and absent-mindedness, I had typed all of this down, never once realising that he was doing this for my sake, and that he had not wished to hurt my feelings by calling attention to the fact that my fingernails were not well cared for, and that the general appearance of my hands could be improved. It did not occur to me until some years later that this had been a device he had used to help me.

Crowley also endeavoured to assist Regardie to overcome his timidity. He advised him temporarily to relinquish his interests in Magic and Mysticism in favour of walking and working his way around the world to familiarize himself with every conceivable vice. As Crowley himself had been inspired to write many years before: 'Go thou into the outermost places and subdue all things. Subdue thy fear and thy disgust. Then – yield!' Regardie did not take this advice and in later life criticized it as all too likely to exacerbate the very fears and guilt it was intended to eradicate. 'I think his insights were superb, but his techniques for dealing with neurotic problems were woefully inadequate.' However, Crowley did insist that Regardie lost his virginity as quickly as possible and more or less ordered him to visit prostitutes.

Yet much to Regardie's surprise, Crowley did not offer to give him any technical instruction in Magic or Yoga. 'I kept on expecting the old man to say: "Right! Show me how you do the Pentagram." But he never did. And I was too shy to bother him.' This was the trouble. Crowley was no longer interested in spoonfeeding earnest young students. He expected them to get on with their work and if there were any problems, he was sure they would demand his help. Under those circumstances, he would have given assistance gladly – but the move had to come from the student. Regardie didn't realize this and was too much in awe of his teacher. So instead Crowley indulged in a favourite hobby of that time, which was devouring detective stories, and Regardie wondered what he was doing wrong and felt neglected. It took him years to understand the dynamics of the situation: ironically enough, he himself was using Crowley's method at the time I came to know him.

Nevertheless, this substantial disappointment did not prevent Regardie from continuing with his magical practices and ferociously studying every Crowley book or unpublished manuscript available at the apartment on Avenue de Suffren, and acquiring an encyclopaedic view of Crowley's output. He was thrilled and inspired by passages from Crowley's Diaries which described personal experiences, such as the following:

When therefore I had made ready the chamber, so that all was dark, save for the Lamp upon the Altar, I began as recorded above, to inflame myself in praying, calling upon my Lord ... And the Chamber was filled with that wondrous glow of ultraviolet light self-luminous, without a source, that hath no counterpart in Nature unless it be in that Dawn of the North ... Then subtly, easily, simply, imperceptibly gliding, I passed away into nothing. And I was wrapped in the black brilliance of my Lord, that interpenetrated me in every part, fusing its light with my darkness, and leaving there no darkness, but pure light. Also I beheld my Lord in a figure and I felt the interior trembling kindle itself into a Kiss – and I perceived the true Sacraments – and I beheld in one moment all the mystic visions in one; and the Holy Grail appeared unto me, and many other inexpressible things were known of me (*John St John*, 1908).

Regardie now had full confirmation that Crowley was, in Francis King's words:

the synthesizer of an occult system of great clarity, consistency, intellectual power and, sometimes, beauty.

The three main strands that Crowley wove into the intricate pattern of his 'Magick' ... were the ritual magic and system of occult correspondences employed by the initiates of the occult fraternity known as the Golden Dawn, the sexo-magical practices of the Order of Oriental Templars, and the religious, historical and philosophical teachings of *The Book of the Law*, an intensely beautiful but often cryptic prose-poem which had, he claimed, been communicated to him by Aiwass in April 1904 (*Introduction* to *Crowley on Christ*).

Mr King is quite right, though there is even more to the matter. Yoga plays a vital part in Crowley's synthesis. An attitude of scepticism is consistently encouraged too; the motto of *The Equinox* was indeed 'The Aim of Religion' but it was equally 'The Method of Science'. Further, Crowley was the greatest occult scholar of the century and made invaluable contributions to the study of Kabbala, Astrology and Tarot.

Regardie took as his magical name The Serpent and explored Crowley's Way, which was structured as a series of Grades. The first is that of Student, whose business it is to acquire a general intellectual knowledge of *all* major systems of attainment. In the ensuing Grade of Probationer, the task is 'to begin such practices as he may prefer and to write a careful record of the same for one year'.[1] On the face of it, this sounds laughably easy. In fact, only a minority survive the course. Their intention arouses every manner of opposition, both within and without themselves.

One who is tough enough to persist becomes a Neophyte, and from now on the Grades correspond to the ten Sephiroth of the Tree of Life of the Kabbalists, a matter which will be explained in its proper place. The principal task of the Neophyte is 'to acquire perfect control of the Astral Plane'.[2] In order to succeed, the Neophyte will have to acquire a fair mastery of basic magical technique and of basic Yoga practices, for on one level, 'perfect control of the Astral Plane' means perfect control of the imagination and unconscious. In the succeeding Grade of Zelator, the main work is to achieve success in Asana and Pranayama. In other words, the aspirant must become a proficient Hatha Yogi, adept in posture and breath control; and the examination is hardly easy:

In examination for physical practices, there is a standardised test. In Asana, for instance, the candidate must remain motionless for a given time, his success being gauged by poising on his head a cup filled with water to the brim; if he spill one drop, he is rejected.[3]

The next stage is that of Practicus who 'is expected to complete his intellectual training, and in particular to study the Kabbala'.[4] He will then be fitted to pass the required test.

In intellectual questions, the candidate must display no less mastery of his subject than if he were entered in the 'final' for Doctor of Science or Law at a first class University ... In the Kabbala, the candidate must discover for himself, and prove to the examiner beyond all doubt, the properties of a number never previously examined by any student.[5]

In the words of another system, he must become adept in Gnana Yoga.

The task of the Philosophus, the following Grade, is 'to complete his moral training'.[6] This moral training is in fact – and at last – undemanding for all who do not suffer from the sickness of guilt. 'Each member must make it his main work to discover for himself his own true will, and to do it, and do nothing else.'[7] The Philosophus is also tested in Devotion to the Order and must succeed in Bhakti Yoga, the Yoga of Love or Devotion to a Deity. There follows an intermediate Grade between Initiate and Adept called Dominus Liminis who 'is expected to show mastery of Pratyahara and Dharana'.[8] In other words, he must become adept in Raja Yoga.

Success here leads to the next Grade of Adeptus Minor (without) who is 'expected to perform the Great Work and to attain the Knowledge and Conversation of the Holy Guardian Angel'.[9] This is the climax; this is the point to which all practices have led. If the Great Work is accomplished, he knows and does his Will and as an Adeptus Minor (within) 'is admitted to the formula of the Rosy Cross on entering the

College of the Holy Ghost'.[10] That is to say that he or she is enabled to practise the highest forms of Sex Magick.

After a period of work, the next Grade of Adeptus Major ensues and here he 'obtains a general mastery of practical Magick, though without comprehension'.[11] This includes 'a proper comprehension of the virtues of perfumes (which) is of the utmost importance to the work of the Adeptus Major, for they constitute the most vital link between the material and astral planes, and it is precisely this link which the Adeptus Major most intimately needs.'[12] One who succeeds in forging this link can proceed to the Grade of Adeptus Exemptus who 'completes in perfection all these matters'[13] and should write a thesis which sets forth his comprehension of the Universe.

There is then a choice. The Exempt Adept can try to hold onto all he has attained, refusing the next ordeal. If so, he becomes a Brother of the Left Hand Path and will ultimately destroy himself. Or he can take the Oath of the Abyss, whereby he 'is stripped of all his attainments and of himself as well, even of his Holy Guardian Angel, and becomes a Babe of the Abyss, who, having transcended the Reason, does nothing but grow in the womb of its mother'.[14] You have to give up all that you have and all that you are. You must die in order to be reborn.

One who succeeds in crossing the Abyss is reborn as a Master of the Temple or Magister Templi. His (or her) task is 'to tend his "garden" of disciples, and to obtain a perfect understanding of the Universe. He is a Master of Samadhi'.[15] Very few human beings have ever attained to the Grade of Magus. It is said that there were eight: Lao Tzu, Siddartha (Gautama Buddha), Krishna, Tahuti (Thoth), Moseh (Moses), Dionysus, Mahmud (Mohammed) and Perdurabo (Crowley), though it is thought that there may have been a few others who aligned their Wills with the Word uttered by the Magus. The Magus 'attains to wisdom, declares his law . . . and is a Master of all Magick in its greatest and highest sense'.[16] The supreme Grade of Ipsissimus 'is beyond all this and beyond all comprehension of those of lower degrees'.[17]

However, Regardie's study of these exalted matters would

be rudely interrupted by the events of March 1929. Back in the United States, the sister who had been such a wet blanket on the eve of Regardie's departure, proceeded to leaf through some of her brother's Crowley books and was utterly appalled. As a result she dashed off to the French Consul in Washington, DC and told him some preposterous story concerning the dreadful dangers to which her naive brother had unwittingly exposed himself. The Consul promised to refer the matter back to Paris for investigation. In consequence Crowley and Regardie came under the scrutiny of the Sûreté Générale. An inspector called at the apartment and it took some time to convince him that a coffee-brewing machine was not in fact some infernal device for distilling drugs. To complicate the issue further, it soon transpired that Regardie had neglected to obtain an identity card. Matters came to a climax owing to further events narrated by Louis Wilkinson in *Seven Friends*:

(Crowley) was offered a substantial sum of money to cast horoscopes for a girl and a man with indications that the two were exceptionally well suited to each other and destined to a happy marriage. This was suggested by a *sale individu* who would have had a considerable commission if the marriage had happened: the girl was rich. Crowley, at that time particularly hard up, refused. The individual then told him that he could and would prevent the renewal of his visa if he did not cast the horoscope. Crowley, knowing that this was so, knowing the man's back-stairs pull with the authorities concerned, still refused . . .

On 8 March 1929 *refus de séjours* were handed out to Crowley for being a German spy and drug addict, to Marie de Miramar for associating with him and to Regardie for associating with him and for not possessing a valid *carte d'identité*. Crowley promptly claimed that he was ill, in order to gain time to institute some form of legal proceedings to reverse the expulsion notices but Marie and Regardie had to leave within twenty-four hours. They took the boat across the English Channel but, despite the fact that Regardie had of course been born in London, they were not permitted to land on British soil on the grounds that as colleagues of Crowley, they were 'undesirable aliens'. Eventually they gained entry to Belgium and went to Brussels.

This expulsion was for me guilt by association, Regardie wrote in *The Eye of the Triangle*. In those days, so massive was my sense of culpability, that I felt as profoundly ashamed of the refus de séjour as if I had actually been guilty of the most heinous crimes. My emotional anguish at that time was considerable.

Crowley's departure from France – for the authorities were wholly unwilling to consider any appeal – was blazoned in the headlines of the international press. On his arrival in England, Colonel Carter of Scotland Yard was anxious enough to visit Gerald Yorke and warn him against Crowley. Yorke responded by setting up a dinner where Carter met Crowley and had a most enjoyable evening. Crowley then set out for Brussels where Regardie awaited his arrival with great apprehension – for during his time with Marie, she had seduced him. The latter was understandably concerned about The Beast's reaction when, inevitably, he would discover the fact – but there was none. In contemporary vernacular, he was totally cool about it.

Regardie stayed in Brussels, typing Crowley's *The Confessions* for ultimate publication, while Crowley and de Miramar went on to Berlin, where they married. The reason for this was to facilitate Marie's entry into Britain, which occurred at the end of the summer. Possibly owing to the good offices of Colonel Carter, Regardie managed to gain entry to England around November 1929 and joined Crowley at the house he had rented at Knockholt in Kent.

It was not a serene household by any means ... [Regardie recalled] I found Crowley ill with a severe bout of phlebitis, while Marie suffered with colitis, boredom and loneliness, and excessive drinking ... Marie coped with her boredom not only through the ingestion of alcohol, but by painting with oils, a pretty messy and unproductive business.[18]

Crowley's principal preoccupation was now The Mandrake Press. Percy Reginald Stephensen, a friend, neighbour and admirer of Crowley's literary gifts, had set it up with his partner, a Mr Goldstein, to publish The Beast's works. *The Stratagem and Other Stories*, a novel entitled *Moonchild*, and the first two volumes of a projected six-volume set of *The Confessions* duly came off the press but most English booksellers wanted nothing whatsoever to do with Crowley. It was proposed to overcome sales resistance by bringing out a defence of the latter, making use of a big scrapbook of book reviews and notices, many of them extremely favourable, which Crowley had assiduously collected over the years. P. R. Stephensen took the credit for writing *The Legend of Aleister Crowley*, though he was substantially assisted throughout by Israel Regardie – who has rightly been credited in subsequent editions. However, in 1939 when the work first appeared, it sold slowly and poorly in spite of its many merits; it failed utterly to eradicate the booksellers' refusal to handle Crowley; and The Mandrake Press ultimately went into liquidation.

Crowley could no longer afford to keep on Regardie as his secretary and so the two men parted amicably. Regardie promptly found employment as secretary to the writer Thomas Burke – notable especially for his powerful tale of horror, *Johnson Looked Back* – enjoyed the experience and forever afterwards looked back on Burke with respect, affection and gratitude, for it was this man who encouraged Regardie to seek a publisher for a manuscript he had written. *A Garden of Pomegranates* duly appeared in 1932 and was succeeded in the same year by *The Tree of Life: A Study in Magic*. We shall look in detail at their contents and consequences in due course. For the present one should note that *A Garden of Pomegranates* has the following dedication: 'To ANKH-AF-NA-KHONSU, the priest of the princes, I gratefully dedicate this work.' This refers to Crowley. It was his magical name as the Scribe who took down *The Book of the Law. The Tree of Life* is dedicated 'with poignant memory of what might have been, to Marsyas'. Again, Marsyas is Crowley in his mystical poem 'AHA!' and Regardie's words display his disappointment in Crowley's apparent neglect of his aspirations. Nevertheless, cordial relations continued, and one can discern a growing confidence in Regardie. For instance, when Crowley wanted to divorce de Miramar and thought that the best way to do that would be if he was the plaintiff, it was Regardie who pointed out the objections.

It is too bad that wasn't thought of several months ago when Maria received your letter stating that you had committed adultery umpteen times and that only the rigours of travelling prevented the number being greater. The letter must have caused you a great deal of pleasure when written, but, alas, it prevents you even thinking of being a plaintiff for divorce now. One can't have it both ways.

It wasn't until roughly five years later in 1937 that the quarrel erupted. Regardie sent Crowley a warm note, enclosing a copy of one of his more recent books. Crowley responded by joking about the name 'Francis', which Regardie had recently taken, threw in some anti-semitic slur and facetiously called him 'Frank'. Regardie was outraged.

His slurs struck a raw nerve. Among my weakest character traits at that time was a sensitivity to criticism, valid or invalid. It still abides with me, though the passing years have attenuated it considerably. But in those days I was inclined to be more hot-headed than I am now, so that I retorted as nastily as I thought he had chided me (*The Eye in the Triangle*).

'Darling Alice,

You really are a contemptible bitch! ...' ran the opening of Regardie's rejoinder, which Crowley took as an inexcusable sneer at his own homosexual tendencies and for which he never forgave Regardie. The revenge of The Beast was particularly unpleasant and consisted of a scurrilous document circulated to Regardie's friends and acquaintances.

Israel Regudy was born in the neighborhood of Mile End Road, in one of the vilest slums in London.

Of this fact he was morbidly conscious, and his racial and social shame embittered his life from the start.

'Regardie' is the blunder of a recruiting sergeant in Washington on the occasion of his brother enlisting in the United States Army. Regudy adopted this error as sounding less Jewish. 'Francis' which he has now taken appears to be a pure invention.

About the year 1924 he began to study the work of, and corresponded with, Mr Aleister Crowley. He put up so plausible an appeal that the latter gentleman paid his passage from America and accepted him as a regular student of Magic.

Apart from his inferiority complex, he was found to be suffering from severe chronic constipation, and measures were taken to cure him of this and also his ingrained habit of onanism.

The cure in the latter case was successful, but Regudy abused his freedom by going under some railway arches and acquiring an intractable gonorrhoea.

Mr Crowley supplied him with shelter, food and clothing for over two years, and was ultimately able to get him a good job as Book-keeper and Secretary to a firm of publishers.

Regudy betrayed, robbed and insulted his benefactor.

For some years his life was somewhat obscure, but he seems to have been wandering for the most part around the West of England as a vagrant, existing on the charity, according to some accounts, of various elderly women; according to others, of some obscure religious orders.

His studies in the Kabbala and Magic enabled him to ingratiate himself with Dion Fortune, who picked him out of his misery and helped him in every possible way.

He betrayed, robbed and insulted his benefactress.

Being now a little more on his feet, he was able to move about more freely, and soon managed to scrape acquaintance with a middle-aged lady occupied in varieties of 'healing' by massage and other devices. He switched over to this form of human activity, and made considerable sums of money. He was thus able to betray, rob and insult his benefactress, go over to America, and start a quackery of his own.

Needless to say, there is barely one word of truth in this horrible libel, which shows Crowley at his most vengeful, vicious and spiteful. Unfortunately, the document had a relatively wide circulation, and as late as 1969, it was mailed to Regardie by an unknown personal enemy. It says much for his courage, integrity and self-confidence that he published the attempted character assassination in full in *The Eye in the Triangle* (1970).

However, from a magical point of view, the consequences were personally devastating. Possibly Regardie had come to look upon Crowley as a father-figure and so was for many years wounded and scarred by this vituperative rejection. He in turn rejected Crowley and repudiated all contact with other Magicians, remaining wholly divorced from the occult movement for very many years.

In due course we shall be exploring Regardie's activities during those years and the developments which eventually led him back to The Beast, though after another manner. His pain and anger can readily be understood. Yet in late maturity, he would look back wryly on his time with 'the wickedest man in the world' and state soberly and sincerely: 'Everything I am today, I owe to him.'

Notes

1 The vast majority of quotations are taken from Crowley's essay *One Star in Sight*, published as an Appendix in *Magick: In Theory and Practice*
2 Ibid.
3 Ibid.
4 Ibid.
5 Ibid.
6 Ibid.
7 Ibid.
8 Ibid.

[9] Ibid.
[10] Ibid.
[11] Ibid.
[12] Crowley, *Seven Seven Seven*, (1907)
[13] Crowley, *One Star in Sight*.
[14] Ibid.
[15] Ibid.
[16] Ibid.
[17] Ibid.
[18] Regardie, Introduction to 2nd edn of *The Legend of Aleister Crowley* (1983).

5

First Fruits

'All sorts of books have been written on the Kabbala, some poor, some few others extremely good,' Regardie wrote in his Introduction to the second edition of *A Garden of Pomegranates*, first published by Rider & Co. in 1932.

But I came to feel the need for what might be called a sort of Berlitz handbook, a concise but comprehensive introduction, studded with diagrams and tables of easily understood definitions and correspondences to simplify the student's grasp of so complicated and abstruse a subject.

During a short retirement in North Devon in 1931, I began to amalgamate my notes. It was out of these that *A Garden of Pomegranates* gradually emerged. I unashamedly admit that my book contains many direct plagiarisms from Crowley, Waite, Eliphas Levi, and D. H. Lawrence. I had incorporated numerous fragments from their works into my notebooks without citing individual references to the various sources from which I condensed my notes ... I was only twenty-four at the time.

Well and good: but what *is* Kabbala? One could do worse than give the answer of the late Dame Frances Yates:

The word means 'tradition'. It was believed that when God gave the Law to Moses He gave also a second revalation as to the secret meaning of the Law. This esoteric tradition was said to have been passed down the ages orally by initiates. It was a mysticism and a cult but rooted in the text of the Scriptures, in the Hebrew language, the holy language in which God had spoken to man (*The Occult Philosophy in the Elizabethan Age*).

During the Renaissance, Kabbala became an integral part of

what was earlier termed The Occult Philosophy, and it is perhaps helpful to remind the reader of certain relevant tenets.

1 All is a Unity, created and sustained by God through His Laws.
2 These Laws are predicated upon Number.
3 There is an art of combining Hebrew letters and equating them with Number so as to perceive profound truths concerning the nature of God and His dealings with Man.
7 According to the Kabbala, God manifests by means of ten progressively more dense emanations: and Man, by dedicating his mind to the study of divine wisdom, by refining his whole being and by eventual communion with the angels themselves, may at last enter into the presence of God.
9 The Universe is an ordered pattern of correspondences: or as Dr Dee put it: 'Whatever is in the Universe possesses order, agreement and similar form with something else (Gerald Suster, *John Dee: Essential Readings*, 1986).

We will recall too how S. L. 'MacGregor' Mathers welded together Renaissance occult philosophy, including and especially the Kabbala, with certain of its sources which had come to light by this time – and his own inspiration – in the creation of the Golden Dawn system. However, the practical use of Kabbala by magicians and mystics has still to be defined and in *Seven Seven Seven*, Aleister Crowley gives the most succinct answer ever written:

Kabbala is
(a) A language fitted to describe certain classes of phenomena and to express certain classes of ideas which escape regular phraseology. You might as well object to the technical terminology of chemistry.
(b) An unsectarian and elastic terminology by means of which it is possible to equate the mental processes of people apparently diverse owing to the constraint imposed upon them by the peculiarities of their literary expression. You might as well object to a lexicon or a treatise on comparative religion.
(c) A system of symbolism which enables thinkers to formulate their ideas with complete precision and to find simple expression for

complex thoughts, especially such as include previously disconnected orders of conception. You might as well object to algebraic symbols.
(d) An instrument for interpreting symbols whose meaning has become obscure, forgotten or misunderstood by establishing a necessary connection between the essence of forms, sounds, simple ideas (such as number) and their spiritual, moral or intellectual equivalents. You might as well object to interpreting ancient art by consideration of beauty as determined by physiological facts.
(e) A system of omniform ideas so as to enable the mind to increase its vocabulary of thoughts and facts through organising and correlating them. You might as well object to the mnemonic value of Arabic modifications of roots.
(f) An instrument for proceeding from the known to the unknown on similar principles to those of mathematics. You might as well object to the use of $\sqrt{}$, -1, x^4 etc.
(g) A system of criteria by which the truth of correspondences may be tested with a view to criticising new discoveries in the light of their coherence with the whole body of truth. You might as well object to judging character and status by educational and social convention.

The basis of the system is a diagram called the Tree of Life. This is a multi-purpose map. It can be used to classify states of consciousness, deities, colours, plants, jewels, the physical body or anything else in the Universe. It is a unifying symbol which embodies the entire cosmos.

It begins with Nothing, which is termed Ain. Ain is unknowable, unthinkable and unspeakable. To render itself comprehensible to itself, Ain becomes Ain Soph (Infinity) and then Ain Soph Aour (Absolute Limitless Light), which concentrates itself into a central dimensionless point. This point is called Kether and it is the first Sephirah (sphere) of the Tree of Life. The Light proceeds to manifest in nine more progressively dense emanations down to the tenth and final Sephirah, Malkuth, the physical world. This, then, is how the Universe manifests, or how God or the Goddess Nuit manifests, or how Darkness becomes Light and then Life – whichever words are preferred – and it is held that every set of phenomena follows this pattern. This is why the Tree of Life is viewed as a multipurpose map.

So our map so far consists of ten Sephiroth. These Sephiroth are connected by twenty-two Paths which express the relations between the Sephiroth they connect. The original creators of the Kabbala attributed the twenty-two letters of the Hebrew alphabet to these Paths and connected them with a symbol, the Serpent of Wisdom, who includes all Paths within its coils as it climbs from the lowest to the highest – which is why Regardie originally took the magical name of The Serpent.

This system has been further expanded and made more complex over the centuries. It is held by most Kabbalists that there are Four Worlds, or dimensions of existence, and each World has its own Tree of Life. Many go further and work with a system whereby each Sephirah contains a Tree, giving us a total of a hundred Trees or, if we bring in the Four Worlds, four hundred. These complexities are beyond the scope of this work but can certainly be studied with advantage in *The Mystical Qabalah* (1935) by Dion Fortune or Regardie's *A Garden of Pomegranates*.

It should be added, however, that there are two ways of regarding Kabbala. The traditionalists believe that the Tree of Life is the framework of the Universe. Crowley disagreed and commented acidly:

> It was as if some one had seriously maintained that a cat was a creature constructed by placing the letters C.A.T. in that order. It is no wonder that Magick has excited the ridicule of the unintelligent, since even its educated students can be guilty of so gross a violation of the first principles of common sense (*Magick: In Theory and Practice*).

His point was that the Tree of Life is a *classification* of the Universe, not a thing in itself. Its unique advantage, or so Crowley, Regardie and other Kabbalists insist, is that it is the most useful tool of universal classification which the mind of Man has ever invented.

During the 1890s, Mathers proceeded to write Tables of the

Tree of Life to classify his vast occult knowledge. Dr Wynn Westcott very probably assisted him and these Tables were circulated among Inner Order initiates, including Allan Bennett. Bennett was an excellent Kabbalist in his own right and Crowley learned from him, then acquired his own experience. A most fruitful result was the publication in 1909 of *Seven Seven Seven*, the classic dictionary of correspondences. As Crowley wrote in his Preface:

> The following is an attempt to systematise alike the data of mysticism and the results of comparative religion.
>
> ...
>
> for us it is left to sacrifice literary charm, and even some accuracy, in order to bring out the one great point.
>
> This: That when a Japanese thinks of Hachiman, and a Boer of the Lord of Hosts, they are not two thoughts, but one.

The main Tables are based on thirty-two numbers: that is, the ten Sephiroth and twenty-two Paths. If we look at the correspondences pertaining to the number five, for example, we will find that the planet is Mars, the Hebrew name is Geburah (Strength), the colour for magical use is scarlet, the Element is Fire, the Egyptian God is Horus, the Greek God Ares, the Roman God Mars, the Hindu deities Vishnu and Varruna-Avatar, the stone is the Ruby, the plants are Oak, Nux Vomica and Nettle, the animals (real and imaginary) are the Phoenix, the Lion and the Child, the metal is Iron, the perfume is Tobacco and so on. One uses *Seven Seven Seven* to set up magical ceremonies, to guide one in meditation and to compare systems of symbolism. Once its basic principles are comprehended, one can classify new knowledge, as Crowley continued to do throughout his life. His work here, based as it was on that of the Golden Dawn and Bennett, has yet to be surpassed and far too many subsequent writers have plundered it without acknowledgement.

By his own admission, Regardie was guilty of this act. Yet it would not be just to dismiss *A Garden of Pomegranates* as mere theft from *Seven Seven Seven*, even though it probably could not have been written were it not for the latter. This would be to miss the work's many merits. *Seven Seven Seven* is not an easy book for the novice and may on first reading leave him or her wholly confounded. *A Garden of Pomegranates* is an ideal introduction to a difficult and complex subject. Moreover, as Regardie wrote in his *Introduction* to the second edition:

The importance of the book to me was and is five-fold. (1) It provided a yardstick by which to measure my personal progress in the understanding of the Kabbala. (2) Therefore it can have an equivalent value to the modern student. (3) It serves as a theoretical introduction to the Kabbalistic foundation of the magical work of the Hermetic Order of the Golden Dawn. (4) It throws considerable light on the occasionally obscure writings of Aleister Crowley. (5) It is dedicated to Crowley, who was the Ankh-af-na-Khonsu mentioned in *The Book of the Law* – a dedication which served both as a token of personal loyalty and devotion to Crowley, but was also a gesture of my spiritual independence from him.

We must now briefly turn our attention to what is known as The Literal Kabbala, the ways of 'combining Hebrew letters and equating them with Number so as to perceive profound truths concerning the nature of God and His dealings with Man'. There are three main methods: Gematria, Notariqon and Temurah. Gematria is the art of discovering the secret sense of a word by means of the numerical equivalents of each letter. As Regardie states in *A Garden of Pomegranates*:

Its method of procedure depends on the fact that each Hebrew letter had a definite numerical value and may actually be used in place of a number. When the total of the numbers of the letters of any one word were identical with that of another word, no matter how different its meaning and translation, a close correspondence and analogy was seen.

He gives us an interesting example. The Hebrew for 'Serpent' adds to 358 and so does the Hebrew for 'Messiah'. This may initially appear surprising but close inspection and a further operation of Gematria will clarify the matter. For what is the Serpent? As Regardie puts it: 'The Serpent is a symbol of the Kundalini, the spiritual creative force in each man which, when aroused by means of a trained will, re-creates the entire individual, making him a God-Man.' And the Messiah is a God-Man. Furthermore, if we add up the digits 3, 5 and 8, we obtain 16, and if we look up the correspondences of the 16th Path in *Seven Seven Seven* or *A Garden of Pomegranates*, we find Dionysius the Redeemer. Another correspondence is that of Parsifal, who becomes able to perform the messianic miracle of redemption. As Regardie states: 'We thus see the specific analogy between the words "Serpent" and "Messiah" which the Kabbala has been able to reveal.'

Notariqon consists essentially of constructing a new word from several words by taking the initial letters of the latter and combining them. In Temurah, the letters of a word are transposed according to various systems to form a new word. These practices concentrate the mind and are believed by their exponents to reveal truths.

It should be stressed that Kabbala is usually found meaningless and even absurd by those with no practical experience of the subject. One cannot learn Kabbala simply by reading about it any more than one can learn chemistry without ever entering a laboratory and performing an experiment. Understanding depends entirely upon and grows with honest work – and any student can be safely advised to study *A Garden of Pomegranates* and imitate the example of Israel Regardie.

Even so, *The Tree of Life: A Study in Magic* is a far more substantial piece of work. Even today, it is regarded as a superb introduction to a way of wisdom which often strikes readers as being difficult and obscure, it is an ideal way of approaching Crowley's more complex writings and, supported as it is by copious quotations from unjustly neglected classical authors, it remains a valuable book in its own right. As Francis King and Isabel Sutherland state in *The Rebirth of Magic*

Crowley had always wanted to write books of magic which could be read and understood by the ordinary reader. He never succeeded in doing this, although he made several efforts to do so. He wrote with great clarity and simplicity on yoga, but his purely magical writings are largely incomprehensible to the reader not equipped with a detailed knowledge of Mathers' qabalistic system the rites of the Golden Dawn, and even the events of Crowley's own life.

The pupil succeeded where the master had failed. In 1932, Regardie published two books, *The Tree of Life* and *The Garden of Pomegranates*, which many consider to be minor occult masterpieces. The former work dealt with the techniques of ritual magic, the latter with the qabalah; in spite of Regardie's close relationship with Crowley they represent the pure Golden Dawn system rather than 'Crowleyanity'. It would seem that, young as he was, Regardie had the discrimination to discern which particular elements of 'Magick' were drawn from, respectively, the OTO, from the *Book of the Law*, and from the Golden Dawn. *The Tree of Life* gives, using alchemical symbolism, a detailed account of the 'Mass of the Holy Ghost' – in other words, the sexual magic of the OTO.

With its detailed and lucid exposition of the how and why of Magic, *The Tree of Life* is an ideal book for the intelligent beginner, and its insights make it valuable also for the advanced student. Such criticisms as can legitimately be made are stylistic. Firstly, there is no humour at all. One has the impression that the author takes both his subject and himself very seriously. Indeed, the late Gerald Yorke recalled with regret in later life his opinion at the time of knowing Regardie that the man had no sense of humour whatsoever. That may have been the case then; or perhaps Regardie was simply very shy and inhibited; but certainly in old age, Regardie was distinguished by a most delightful sense of humour. Even so and by his own later admission, he never managed to impart it to his writings.

Secondly, and again by its author's later admission, *The Tree of Life* is mannered in its execution. Because Regardie was painfully conscious of his lack of a formal university education, he endeavoured to compensate for this by the adoption of a weighty and occasionally ponderous prose style. Years would pass before he had sufficient confidence to write simply, clearly and cleanly: nevertheless, his early manner does not mar the excellence of his content nor does it interfere with judicious appreciation.

The publication of his first two books had a number of interesting consequences. *The Tree of Life* was acidly reviewed in the London *Saturday Review* under the heading 'The Way of Madness', by 'A Student of Life' who was in fact the editor, a Mr H. Warner Allen. This review elicited a response from a psychiatrist which was published in the issue of 10 December 1932.

Having read with the greatest possible interest and approval *The Tree of Life* by Israel Regardie, I was surprised by the lack of insight shown in his criticism by 'A Student of Life'. Largely by the experience of patients and of my own, and a little by the study of the written works of others, I have gradually discovered a little about life. It was with amazement and the joy of meeting a friend in a strange land that I read Mr Regardie's book and found that the little I had discovered was a very small part of that very elaborate system which he has enunciated in his book with so much simplicity. My own method has always been the scientific one, and I was deeply impressed that his was the same, but where I was only a beginner he has shown me the way to further progress in my search for understanding.

Your reviewer is confused and unfair, but Mr Regardie is neither. I write hoping that the intelligent reader may not be put off by an unintelligent review from reading a work of great significance and value. It is not one which can be readily appreciated by all because of the inherent difficulty of its subject, but there are many to whom it would come as a ray of light on a dark road.

The writer was E. Graham Howe, MD, uncle of Ellic Howe – the author of some curious works on the history of magical orders which unite detailed, dogged and painstaking research with a puzzling hostility to Magic. Dr Graham Howe made the acquaintance of Regardie and it is possible that this stimulated the latter's subsequent interest in and involvement with the world of psychology. Certainly Regardie liked him and he seems to have been a remarkable individual. I have heard another extraordinary man, Gerard Noel, among other things the editor of a first-class periodical called *Pentagram*, give unstinting praise to the memory of Dr Howe of whom he declared: 'Everything I am today, I owe to him.'

Regardie also made the acquaintance of the celebrated Magician, Dion Fortune, whose books he greatly admired. Unfortunately, he found her disappointing in person. 'Mind you, most authors are,' he added ruefully when I first met him. A fairly recent and interesting work, *Dancers To The Gods* by Alan Richardson, has given credit for much of Dion Fortune's achievements to her husband, Dr Penry-Evans, who was apparently a tower of strength and a pillar of support. Regardie did not concur with this opinion, dismissing the good doctor with the words: 'Never seen a man so bloody hen-pecked.'

Even so, he enjoyed cordial relations with Dion Fortune, who greeted his books with enthusiasm and argued that much occult secrecy was unnecessary. This was hardly the view of a representative of a Golden Dawn offshoot, the Alpha et Omega Lodge. According to Francis King and Isabel Sutherland:

> Captain E. J. Langford-Garstin wrote to him demanding that he should never again mention the name of the Golden Dawn in print; occult secrecy, he affirmed, was all-important. Dion Fortune took the opposite point of view ... A representative of the Stella Matutina, presumably a schizophrenic, managed to hold both points of view at the same time and wrote to both Langford-Garstin and Dion Fortune expressing full agreement with their respective positions. Unfortunately the letters were inserted in the wrong envelopes (*The Rebirth of Magic*).

The controversy provoked by Regardie's books led to meetings with representatives of the Stella Matutina – another Golden Dawn offshoot – most notably a Mrs Hughes. In 1934, a new phase of his life commenced when he was admitted to this magical Order.

6

The Golden Dawn and a Poison Cloud

Why did the Golden Dawn play so central a part in the lives of both Crowley and Regardie? To recapitulate: Magic is a way of perfecting the various faculties of Man and raising him in stages to Godhead. In the course of doing it, the Magician gains understanding of various subtle processes of Nature and comes into contact with beings who may or may not exist independently of the unconscious mind. It is argued by Magicians that everything in the Universe is connected with everything else in an ordered pattern of correspondences. The paraphernalia employed in magical rituals – the circle, triangle, wands, cups, swords, disks, robes, lamens etc. – these are means of manipulating correspondences, enflaming the imagination and focusing the will into a blazing stream of pure energy. Although branches of Magic deal with practical, material matters, the fundamental goal is the attainment of superconsciousness, enabling the Magician to know and accomplish his true purpose in life. This is the High Magic to which the Golden Dawn Order was dedicated.

The origins of the Order are still a matter for dispute. The controversy can be studied in Ellic Howe's *The Magicians of the Golden Dawn* (1972) in which it is skilfully argued that the Order was founded on a fraud; and the present writer's *Suster's Answer to Howe* (in Regardie's *What You Should Know About the Golden Dawn*, 1983) which raises questions Howe has failed to consider and arrives at a verdict of not proven. Since the appearance of the latter, there has been another edition of Mr Howe's book, containing a new Introduction which takes notice of *Suster's Answer*. Unfortunately, instead of tackling sensibly the questions raised by my essay, Mr Howe chooses instead to abuse it without providing any supporting evidence. It is disappointing to note that personal animosity has entered into the controversy and prevents objective consideration of the questions at issue.

A third possibility in the origins controversy has been suggested in private conversation by Eric Towers and others, including the noted authority on Magic and the Golden Dawn, Francis King. This is that a Dr Westcott did indeed forge documents which purported to give the Golden Dawn a 'Rosicrucian' and Continental origin but that 'MacGregor' Mathers nevertheless subsequently brought through genuine Magic. This possibility should be seriously considered.

In the end, of course, the question of origins is of purely academic interest. Either Golden Dawn Magic works or it doesn't. There is no dispute that the Order was founded on the basis of a set of cipher manuscripts. Absolutely nobody knows or claims to know where these came from originally. Neither is it disputed that they came into the possession of Dr W. Wynn Westcott, a London coroner, probably in 1887. Westcott asked an occult scholar, S. L. 'MacGregor' Mathers to assist him. The code was a relatively simple one, contained in *Polygraphiae* by John Trithemius and the manuscripts turned out to contain skeletonic rituals of a loosely 'Rosicrucian' nature and the address of one Fraulein Sprengel in Nuremberg. Westcott claimed that he wrote to her, receiving in return a Charter to found the Golden Dawn.

Howe and his followers have alleged that Sprengel never existed and that Westcott forged the Charter and letters from Germany, but the controversy is not germane here. The facts remain that Mathers expanded and wrote up the skeletonic rituals and these were duly enacted in temples set up in London, Edinburgh, Bradford, Weston-super-Mare, and later, Paris.

In 1891, Westcott claimed that Sprengel had died and her associates had broken off all communication, urging the Golden Dawn leaders to form their own links with 'the Secret Chiefs', allegedly superhuman beings concerned with the spiritual evolution of mankind. In Paris 1892 Mathers claimed to have established these links. A second, inner and

'Rosicrucian' Order was founded; The Red Rose and the Cross of Gold, and page after page of theoretical and practical occult teaching flowed from the clairvoyantly inspired pen of Mathers. Yet the resulting system was beautiful and possessed bewildering yet logically coherent complexity. For Mathers had welded together an amalgam of traditions drawn from the Magic of Egypt and Chaldea, the Hebrew Kabbala, the Tarot and medieval and Renaissance esotericism together with his own inspiration into a body of knowledge and a method for taking practical advantage of that knowledge.

Unfortunately, as time went on, the London members grew weary of the autocratic manner of Mathers. Although many of them were perfectly ordinary people whom Aleister Crowley snobbishly dismissed as nonentities, there were some notable initiates: W. B. Yeats, the poet; Arthur Machen and Algernon Blackwood, the writers; George Cecil Jones, chemist, metallurgist and accomplished Magician; Allan Bennett, later Bhikku Ananda Metteya, who would in time bring Buddhism to England; J. W. Brodie-Innes, novelist; Florence Farr, actress and intimate of Bernard Shaw; Maud Gonne, whose beauty and Irish revolutionary fervour inspired Yeats; and Mrs Oscar Wilde. Mathers, who had for some time been living in Paris with his wife Moina, sister of the philosopher Henri Bergson, responded by becoming still more autocratic. Letters were exchanged between London and Paris – the various issues involved lie beyond the scope of this work – and accusations were hurled until, at the end of March 1900, the London Temple declared its independence of its creator. As we have noted, Aleister Crowley promptly dashed off to Paris, pledged his loyalty to Mathers and returned to London as the latter's Envoy Plenipotentiary.

There was then a magical duel between Yeats and Crowley, succinctly recorded by Francis King and Isabel Sutherland in their delightful history, *The Rebirth of Magic*:

(Yeats) claimed that the Order wonder-workers had 'called up' one of Crowley's mistresses on the astral plane and told her to betray her lover. Two days later, said Yeats, she spontaneously approached a member of the Order and offered to go to Scotland Yard and give evidence of 'torture and medieval iniquity'. Crowley's diary gave quite a different account of this psychic attack – his ornamental Rose Cross turned white, while fires refused to burn in his lodgings; his rubber mackintosh spontaneously went up in flames, for no apparent reason he lost his temper, and on at least five occasions horses bolted at the sight of him.

Crowley replied by seizing the Order's premises with the aid of some toughs he had hired at a pub in Leicester Square ... The triumph was only a temporary one. With the aid of the police, the Second Order regained control of its premises and, for good measure, managed to persuade one of Crowley's creditors to issue a writ against him.

While all this was going on in London Mathers was resorting to black magic in Paris. He had taken a large packet of dried peas, baptised each pea with the name of one of his opponents, invoked the devils Beelzebub and Typhon-Set and had then, simultaneously shaking the peas in a large sieve, called upon these dark gods to confound the rebels with quarrels and discord. This seems to have been one of the most successful curses ever recorded, for having got rid of Mathers the members of the Golden Dawn spent the next few years quarrelling violently with one another.

The Order fragmented into factions. One was the Rosicrucian Order of the Alpha et Omega (AO), which consisted of those who remained loyal to Mathers or after a period of rebellion, returned to their original allegiance. The AO had a Temple in Paris under Mathers, one in London under Dr Berridge, a homeopath and disciple of Thomas Lake Harris, and some American Temples chartered by Mathers prior to 1900. In 1911 J. W. Brodie-Innes, who had taken a leading part in the original revolt, resumed contact with Mathers, received 'new and exceedingly powerful formulae' from him and revived the dormant Edinburgh Temple, Amen-Ra, under the authority of the Alpha et Omega.

In November 1918 Mathers died in the world-wide epidemic of Spanish influenza and was succeeded by his wife

Moina, who chartered some more American temples before her own death in the 1920's. Brodie-Innes also died at that time but the AO continued. Its moving spirit was Captain E. J. Langford-Garstin, the man who rebuked Regardie for revealing magical 'secrets' in his books, but Garstin met with financial disaster and committed suicide and it appears that, soon after, the AO became dormant.

A second faction was the 'Holy' Order of the Golden Dawn led by A. E. Waite, who rewrote the rituals, lengthened them intolerably, Christianized them and removed the magical elements. Eventually Waite left his own fraternity because of what he called 'internecine feuds over documents' and it died a richly deserved death.

A third was led by Crowley, who announced in *The Equinox* that his A .·. A .·. included the Golden Dawn – the GD, he claimed, was the Outer College for the Grades Neophyte to Philosophus – and published inaccurate versions of its initiatory rituals and accurate renditions of its teachings in addition to his own superb innovations. However, although Crowley's synthesis was heavily influenced by the Golden Dawn *system*, one cannot say that he was running a Golden Dawn *Order*.

The fourth faction is the most important one for our present purposes. This was the Stella Matutina led by Dr R. W. Felkin, a former Christian missionary in Uganda and an expert in tropical medicine. In 1912 Dr and Mrs Felkin chartered a new Temple in New Zealand, to which they emigrated four years later. This Temple still flourishes today under Mr Pat Zalaski. And shortly before their final departure from England, the Felkins chartered three new temples in this country: one was intended for Freemasons and little is known of its activities or lack of them; one was for A. E. Waite, the Master devoid of a Temple, and next to nothing was accomplished; and the third was situated in Bristol 'and was led by occultists experienced in the Golden Dawn magical tradition'.[1]

Felkin's own London Temple, Amoun, had as its moving spirits Dr W. Hammond, a chief of the Stella Matutina Masonic Temple; the Reverend F. N. Heazall, an Anglican clergyman; and Miss C. M. Stoddart. These three chiefs neglected disciplined magical work in favour of sloppy spiritualist-style mediumship and the Temple collapsed. Subsequently Miss Stoddart became obsessed with the idea of a sinister world-wide conspiracy of Freemasons, Jews and Golden Dawn members and her book, *Light-Bearers of Darkness* under the pseudonym 'Inquire Within' can still delight lovers of intellectual fatuity.

The Masonic Temple, which was also strongly influenced by the ideas of Rudolf Steiner, eventually expired; so the sole GD Temple which could be described as 'flourishing' during the 1930's was The Stella Matutina Hermes Temple in Bristol, which Regardie joined. One of its more notable initiates was Professor C. D. Broad, the Cambridge philosopher and author of *The Mind And Its Place In Nature*; and in due course the Order would be joined by Dr E. Graham Howe.

Obviously Regardie was excited by the prospect of becoming part of so distinguished a Magical Order, the teachings of which had had so profound an effect upon Crowley. For the Golden Dawn system can be regarded as the supreme harmonious synthesis of classical techniques. Its object is to bring the individual to a blazing consciousness of the white light of the divine spirit within. The process of doing this is called Initiation.

Those who practise the Golden Dawn system believe that honourably intentioned and technically sound magical work accomplished by an Order gives its officers the power to arouse this 'white light of the divine spirit' in others through beautiful but complex magical ceremonies. This is achieved in stages and by degrees. Unlike the A .·. A .·. Way, there are no such Grades as Student or Probationer. The aspirant commences the quest by undergoing the Neophyte Ritual. This is of fundamental importance, for by it the magical potential of the individual is activated. As Crowley states in *Magick: In Theory and Practice*:

This formula has for its 'first matter' the ordinary man entirely ignorant of everything and incapable of anything. He is therefore represented as blindfolded and bound. His only aid is his aspiration, represented by the officer who is to lead him into the Temple. Before entering, he must be purified and consecrated. Once within the Temple, he is required to bind himself by an oath. His aspiration is now formulated as Will. He makes the mystic circumambulation of the Temple. After further purification and consecration, he is allowed for one moment to see the Lord of the West, and gains courage to persist. For the third time he is purified and consecrated, and he sees the Lord of the East, who holds the balance, keeping him in a straight line. In the West he gains energy. In the East he is prevented from dissipating the same. So fortified, he may be received into the order as a neophyte by the three principal officers, thus uniting the Cross with the Triangle. He may then be placed between the pillars of the Temple, to receive the fourth and final consecration. In this position the secrets of the grade are communicated to him, and the last of his fetters is removed. All this is sealed by the sacrament of the Four Elements.

It will be seen that the *effect of this whole ceremony is to endow a thing inert and impotent with balanced motion in a given direction.*

The newly inducted Neophyte then studies the language and grammar of Magick and undertakes elementary practices such as meditation. The next stage is the successive taking of the Four Elemental Grades. The Four Elements of the Ancients – Fire, Water, Air and Earth – are held to correspond with, among other things, states of human consciousness which need to be aroused and activated. Earth, Air, Water and Fire correspond with Malkuth, Yesod, Hod and Netzach, the four lowest Sephiroth on the Tree of Life. Hence, in the next Grade of Zelator the candidate steps into Malkuth and the initiatory ritual is designed to activate his energies of Earth. What on earth is meant by this phrase: 'the energies of Earth'? Simply, those fundamental characteristics in the human psyche to which we refer when we make a statement like: 'John and Jane are very down to earth.' One effect of the Zelator initiation should be the increase of common sense and animal strength on the part of the aspirant.

Further study and further practice follow before the Theoricus initiation, the Practicus intiation, and the Philosophus initiation, which work on bringing out further elemental energies of humankind: imagination, intellect and emotion. This is in order to maximize all aspects of human potential which are usually repressed by the conscious ego or suppressed by external society, and to balance them in perfect harmony. It is intended that the Magician will think with his brain, feel with his heart, lust with his guts and stand with his feet firmly on the ground: far too many in ordinary life muddle the matter and, for instance, lust with their brains, endeavour to stand firmly on the swirling tides of emotion, think with their guts and allow feelings to dictate where they put their feet. This wastes energy and prevents healthy psychological integration, leading to endless self-destructive, internal conflicts.

It is held by Golden Dawn initiates that if the work appropriate to each Grade has been seriously undertaken and the initiatory ceremonies properly performed, then the energized aspirant is ready for the next important stage, the Portal Grade, but only after seven months of meditating on what has gone before and absorbing its effects. This is no easy business. As Crowley writes:

> the Aspirant, on the Threshold of Initiation, finds himself assailed by the complexes which have corrupted him, their externalisation excruciating him, and his agonised reluctance to their elimination plunging him into such ordeals that he seems (both to himself and to others) to have turned from a noble and upright man into an unutterable scoundrel (*Magick: In Theory and Practice*).

And as Regardie states:

> The significance of all this is to point to a higher type of consciousness, the beginning of a spiritual rebirth. It acts as a self-evolved link between the higher Self at peace in its eternal place, and the human soul, bound by its fall to the world of illusion, fear and anxiety. But until that self-awareness and acquired knowledge are turned to higher and initiated goals, sorrow and anxiety are the

inevitable results. In other words, it will not do for the Adept to be cut off from his roots. He must unite all the component parts of his mind-body system and integrate every element on the Tree, his own organism. He must develop by use, the titanic forces of his unconscious psyche so that they may become as a powerful but docile beast whereon he may ride. The personality must be reorganized on an entirely new basis. Every element therein demands equilibration so that illumination ensuing from magical work may not give rise to fanaticism and pathology instead of Adeptship and integrity. Balance is required for the accomplishment of the Great Work. 'Equilibrium is the basis of the soul.' (*The Eye in the Triangle*).

After the Portal Grade, in which the four activated Elements are balanced and crowned with the Element of Spirit, nine months must pass before the aspirant can approach the Inner Order for the beautiful and important intiation into the sephirah of Tiphareth and the Grade of Adeptus Minor. Here there is a symbolic death and resurrection, and the candidate is reborn as an Adept who has beheld the Godhead. The next task is the mastery of magical technology, some of which includes the arousal and control of magical power or 'light' or 'the energy of the Spirit' within the self so as to transfer it to other aspirants during their ceremonies of initiation.

The attentive reader may have noticed that there are other ways of regarding this initiatory process. For example, one could accept the hypothesis that the human psyche consists of 'a ladder of selves' – as Colin Wilson and others have suggested – and that each step on this ladder makes one conscious of a deeper self within until one comes to the Self that is the highest. Some would call this 'God within us' – Hindus call it *atman*, which is the same – and Crowley came to call it the True Will.

Another schema involves postulating that magical and mystical progress consists of becoming conscious of and then stripping away the various thick veils of falsehood which surround and smother that Spirit or Will which we are.

Under the Golden Dawn system, the Adeptus Minor has to

tackle a vast body of work: this could easily take a lifetime. Assuming this is accomplished, he is raised merely to a sub-Grade of Adeptus Minor; and yet more work has to be done. Here is the programme:

Part One. A. Preliminary. Receive and copy: Notes on the Obligation. The Ritual of the 5 = 6 Grade (Adeptus Minor). The manuscript. Sigils from the Rose. The Minutum Mundum. Having made your copies of these and returned the originals you should study them in order to prepare to sit for the written examination. You must also arrange with the Adept in whose charge you are, about your examination in the Temple on the practical work.

Part Two. Receive the Rituals of the Pentagram and Hexagram. Copy and learn them. You can now sit for the written examination in these subjects and complete 'A' by arranging to be tested in your practical knowledge in the Temple.

Part One. B. Implements. Receive the Rituals of the Lotus Wand, Rose-Cross, Sword, and the Elemental Weapons. Copy and return them. There is a written examination on the above subjects – that is on the construction, symbolism, and use of these objects, and the general nature of a consecration ceremony and the forming of invocations. This can be taken before the practical work of making is begun or at any stage during it.

Part Two. This consists in the making of the Implements which must be passed as suitable before the consecration is arranged for, in the presence of a Chief or other qualified Adept. The making and consecration are done in the order given above unless it is preferred to do all the practical work first, and make arrangements for consecration as convenient.

Part One. G. Neophyte Formulae. Receive and copy Z.1. on the symbols and formulae of the Neophyte Ritual. z.3. the symbolism of Neophyte in this Ceremony. Copy the God-form designs of the Neophyte Ritual. The written examination on the Z. manuscripts may now be taken.

Part Two. To describe to the Chief or other suitable Adept in the Temple the arrangement of the Astral Temple and the relative positions of the Forms in it. To build up any God-form required, using the correct Coptic Name.

Thus the work of the first sub-Grade, that of Zelator Adeptus Minor. The work of the Theoricus Adeptus Minor follows:

Part One. C. Psychic. This consists in a written examination in the Tatwa system. Its method of use, and an account of any one vision you have had from any card.

Part Two. This consists in making a set of Tatwa cards, if you have not already done so, and sending them to be passed by the Chief or other Adept appointed. To take the examiner on a Tatwic journey, instructing him as if he were a student and vibrating the proper names for a selected symbol.

Part One. D. Divination. Receive and study the Tarot system, making notes of the principal attributions of the Inner method.

Part Two. Practical. On a selected question, either your own, or the examiner's, to work out a Divination first by Geomancy, then by Horary Astrology, then by the complete Inner Tarot system, and send in a correlated account of the result.

Part One. F. Angelic Tablets. Receive and make copies of the Enochian Tables, the Ritual of the Concourse of the Forces, and the Ritual of the making of the Pyramids, Sphinx, and God-form for any square. A written examination on these subjects may now be taken.

Part Two. Make and colour a pyramid for a selected square, and to make the God-form and Sphinx suitable to it, and to have this passed by an Adept. To prepare a Ritual for practical use with this square, and in the presence of a Chief or other Adept appointed to build it up astrally and describe the vision produced. To study and play Enochian chess, and to make one of the Chess boards and a set of Chessmen.

Part One. E. Talismans. Receive a manuscript on the making and consecrating of Talismans. Gather Names, Sigils, etc., for a Talisman for a special purpose. Make a design for both designs of it and send it in for a Chief to pass. Make up a special ritual for consecreating to the purpose you have in mind and arrange a time with the Chief for the Ceremony of Consecration.

This completes the work of a Theoricus Adeptus Minor.

The sub-Grades of Practicus Adeptus Minor and Philosophus Adeptus Minor which follow, are still more demanding.

It is therefore hardly surprising to note Regardie's view that anyone who openly claims any Grade above Adeptus Minor, 'by that very act raises a gigantic question mark against the validity of the attainment'.

Taking the magical Name of Ad Majorem Adonai Gloriam, Israel Regardie made very rapid progress through the lower Grades of the Order. He had been intimately familiar with the material there for a number of years. He swiftly attained the Grade of Zelator Adeptus Minor – and yet it was in a state of bitter disillusionment with the Order. He condemned its Chiefs for perverting a noble system. He was disappointed in and disgusted by their approach to the rituals.

> As a result the ceremony which was conducted on behalf of the whole fraternity was dead. The Temple never became enlivened with the flashing force that should have manifested itself. No power was generated in any way. The ceremony became a meaningless perfunctory piece of formalism, the Chief Adept simply mumbling his speeches as though anxious to be through with it, and nothing more (*What You Should Know about the Golden Dawn*).

Worse, the Chiefs were obsessed both with Grades and with their own importance. One claimed to be an Adeptus Exemptus while another had the audacity to claim that of Magus.

> It is to such ridiculous heights of vanity and fantasy that the members were sometimes accustomed to look for advice and guidance ... Yet, ironically enough, frequent conversations and repeated enquiries for information concerning fundamental issues of the mere Adeptus Minor work, elementary stuff one would have thought, elicited not the least satisfaction ... The root of the trouble, quite apart from the grade misconceptions as well as the curse of vanity, was of course that the work was only cursorily performed. No one really cared a fig for Magic and spiritual development. No one really strived for mastery of any technique. Grades, and grades alone, were the goal (Ibid.).

The present-day Chiefs have been so ashamed secretly of their lack of ability, and their absence of magical initiative and pioneering spirit, as well as of the puerility of their intellectual outlook in connection with the traditional technique, that they engineered unconsciously a revenge upon the Order. As compensation for their own futility, for their own psychic and spiritual deficiencies, they have foisted upon the whole Order the paucity of their own attainment. They have projected their inferiority upon their subordinates by refusing to acknowledge any intelligence either past or present keener than their own. In the presence of practical work suggesting initiative or the experimental spirit they have responded solely with cheap sneers and cynicisms. Under the hypocritical and, in my estimation, dogmatic guise of scepticism which was cultivated ostensibly to protect students from the dangers of dogma, they have with-held every scrap of useful material having an experimental origin and which might be serviceable as establishing valid and primary principles of Magical practice (Ibid.).

This placed Regardie in an agonizing dilemma. He believed absolutely in the nobility and efficaciousness of the Golden Dawn system, he thought that it had the potential to regenerate the consciousness of thousands of indivuduals, and yet it was now choking to death in the grubby hands of vain and witless Inepti. The only way to save it was surely to make the teachings available to all seekers after wisdom; but this would involve breaking the oath of secrecy which Regardie had sworn. After much excruciating thought, he signed away any financial gains which might accrue to him and resolved to publish the Golden Dawn system, taking openly upon himself full responsibility for the breach of his oath. In February 1935 he completed his prefatory book, *My Rosicrucian Adventure*, subsequently republished as *What You Should Know about the Golden Dawn*:

A torrent of malicious slander was let loose after the publication of my *Tree of Life*, and quite wrongfully I was calumniated, vilified and slandered. And for no adequate reason that I can see. No obligations were broken, and certainly no smirch was reflected upon the divine Theurgy which to me was, and still is, the only thing worthwhile in life and living. Even more calumny may be released by the issue of this preliminary publication, like black qliphotic ravens with vilification beneath their wings. But that is not my concern ... If I have wronged the Order, its guardians will know how and where and in what way I may be punished. If I am guilty of treachery and have mistakenly worked against the intent and purpose of the true occult forces behind the Golden Dawn, those intelligent powers concerned with the initiation of mankind, then willingly I open myself to the avenging punitive current. On the other hand, there is little doubt but that I may expect every assistance in this my venture of publication should those guardians also feel that the Order has finished its day. Herein and deliberately, by this very act, do I, Ad Majorem Adonai Gloriam, Zelator Adeptus Minor R.R. et A.C., invoke that same guardian of the Mysteries before whom I sincerely swore, when bound on the Cross of Obligation, that I would devote myself to the Great Work, and that always and at all times shall I have the best interests of that work at heart. And if I fail herein, and if my present act be contrary to the true intent of whatever divine powers may be, willingly let my 'Rose be blasted and my power in Magic cease.'

Between 1938 and 1940 the Aries Press of Chicago published four volumes of Golden Dawn material edited by Regardie.

'For many years, in spite – or perhaps because – of its excellence, this compilation sold very slowly,' write Francis King and Isabel Sutherland in *The Rebirth of Magic*. 'Almost twenty years after its first publication it was still in print and was available from London's leading occult bookseller.'

Regardie was indeed vilified as a result; and some of his enemies even resorted to magical attack, a notion which always aroused his scorn. 'I received so many curses, I could've papered my walls with them,' he told me; 'That was about all they were fit for.' Gradually, though, there was a growth of appreciation, as R. A. Gilbert has stated:

By the time the fourth volume had appeared in 1940 many members of the Stella Matutina had become reconciled to the work – if only for the practical reason that the existence of a printed ritual removed the need for manual copying. A further result of his action was the birth of 'The Brothers of the Path,' a movement founded in Yorkshire by Anthony Greville-Gascoigne; it was inspired by Regardie's works, devoted to the promotion of his type of occultism, and it published a journal called *The Golden Dawn*, to which Regardie contributed a justification of his work. But the journal, the Brotherhood and its ideals all vanished in the Second World War (*The Golden Dawn: Twilight of the Magicians*).

The Hermes Temple of the Stella Matutina staggered on, on occasion enjoying periods when good magical work was done, but died with its last chief in 1972. That meant that with the exception of the 'Smaragdum Thalasses' Temple, the New Zealand fraternity founded by Dr Felkin, there was no longer any legitimate descendant of the Golden Dawn.[2] What there was, however, was a system which anyone could buy in book form and which could be put into practice by individuals and groups. Moreover, there was therein a mine of magical information from which other Orders could draw. Since the late 1950s, many books on Magic have been published which on examination turn out to be little more than pieces of extrapolation from Regardie's *The Golden Dawn*, accompanied by their authors' largely uninteresting comments. The most important result of Regardie's action has been ably summarized by Francis King and Isabel Sutherland:

In the early 1950's there was a mild revival of interest in ritual magic, presumably sparked off by the publication of John Symonds' biography and C. R. Cammell's memoir of Aleister Crowley. The price of second-hand copies of the latter's books began to rise and individual occultists began to experiment with the techniques taught in those books. Some of these latter found the traditional Western magic embedded in Crowley's system to be of more interest to them than either OTO sex magic or the new religion of Thelema and diverted their attention to the Golden Dawn. They studied Regardie's writings and more popular occult manuals which taught simplified Golden Dawn techniques, such as those written by the late W. E. Butler, a one-time pupil of Dion Fortune.

Eventually these individual practitioners of ceremonial magic began to come together and form new occult brotherhoods in both Britain and the USA. Sometimes such fraternities have claimed to be 'derived from the Golden Dawn' or 'older than the Golden Dawn', but not one of them has produced evidence to satisfactorily confirm these claims. It is probable, therefore, that they are all based on literary sources – primarily the writings of Israel Regardie. This does not mean, of course, that what is taught by these organisations is valueless, nor that they do not number amongst their members occultists who have travelled far along the road of magical attainment (*The Rebirth of Magic*).

In due course we shall be looking at Regardie's postwar influence on magical organizations and at his further contributions to the Golden Dawn system. For the present, however, it is best to return to *The Rebirth of Magic* and the truthful verdict rendered by King and Sutherland:

That the rebirth of occult magic has taken place in the way it has can be very largely attributed to the writings of one man, Dr Francis Israel Regardie.

Notes

1 Francis King and Isabel Sutherland, *The Rebirth of Magic* (1982). I am greatly indebted to this work for my summary of Golden Dawn history and recommend it without any hesitation. King's *Ritual Magic in England: 1887 to the Present Day* also blends agreeable wit with ripe scholarship.

It can be fascinating to compare and contrast the various accounts of Golden Dawn history and the attitudes behind them. Ellic Howe's *The Magicians of the Golden Dawn: A Documentary History of a Magical Order* (1972) is valuable for the meticulous and painstaking research of its author Regardie's *What You Should Know about the Golden Dawn* (1983), which contains my *Suster's Answer to Howe*, is also essential reading here. *The Unicorn* (year) by Virginia Moore gives an account of the Order from the point of view of W. B. Yeats. *The Golden Dawn: Twilight of the Magicians* (1985) by R. A. Gilbert is skilfully researched and though there is little new material of interest, the account serves as a useful supplement to the work of Ellic Howe.

In *Crowley's Apprentice*, it was not necessary, in my view, to do anything more than sketch the broad, rough outline of Golden Dawn history. Serious students of the issues involved will find all the details one could desire in the works of Ellic Howe and R. A. Gilbert, though they will be puzzled by the ignorance of practical magic and hostility to their subject-matter which these authors display beneath a guise of scholarly objectivity.

Perhaps the matter is summed up in Mr Gilbert's curious subtitle to his *The Golden Dawn – Twilight of the Magicians*. Twilight, of course, is not at dawn but at dusk. One wonders what Regardie would say as he brought his psychoanalytical acumen to bear upon this elementary error – for Golden Dawn Temples, as Mr Gilbert knows, are still flourishing.

[2] For those interested in the matter, there is a tangled, complex and obscure mass of questions concerning American Golden Dawn lineage. Mathers chartered some Temples in the United States prior to 1900 and may have chartered more later; we don't know what happened to them. Moina Mathers is alleged to have sold charters to Americans after 1918; if so, what became of them? Felkin, Brodie-Innes or (unfortunately) Waite may, for all we know, have given, granted or sold charters to Americans.

The present writer is not aware of any American GD Temple which claims direct descent from an English GD Temple. Such lineage as is claimed derives from the New Zealand Temple founded by Dr and Mrs Felkin. Of particular interest here is the Georgia Temple. One hears that good GD work is done there and one would like to know where it came from.

But in fact, isn't the issue of charters an extremely boring one? Who really cares? If a group is doing good magical work, it doesn't need a charter. If it isn't doing good magical work, then even a charter won't save it.

7

On the Couch

Regardie's involvement in Magic was meanwhile given a new and deeper perspective by his growing intellectual passion for psychology. In addition to his voracious reading and ensuing reflection, he studied psychoanalysis with Dr E. Clegg and Dr J. L. Bendit, received training in the Jungian system, underwent Freudian analysis and became a lay analyst. Here we can detect a number of considerations which impelled his investigations.

One was a simple, ravenous hunger after knowledge and wisdom. A second was his adherence to the ancient Greek maxim: 'Know Thyself'; the purpose of psychoanalysis. A third was his search for methods which could transform the cramped and inhibited psyche so as to produce a liberated and fully integrated individual, one who lived the maxim: 'Be Thyself'. He had thought that this was to be found in Magic but so many of his fellow-initiates in the Stella Matutina had horrified him. Despite all their grandiose claims, they were wholly lacking in elementary self-knowledge: Magic had done little for them other than inflate and exacerbate egos already sufficiently swollen. Moreover, despite his own magical attainments, remarkable in a man not yet twenty-eight, he remained acutely aware of his own shortcomings and driven by the desire to dissolve the complexes which still blocked the full and healthy expression of the energies within him. Finally, he was plagued by asthma, the occupational disease of occultists, and this drove him to seek relief via psychoanalysis.

What *is* psychoanalysis? The life of its founder, Sigmund Freud (1856–1939), is too well known to bear repetition here; yet even today one encounters extraordinary misconceptions as to the nature of Freud's teachings and even regarding the use of elementary terms. One hopes that one will be forgiven for beginning with basics and stating that *psychology* is the science of the mind and of human behaviour; that *psychiatry* is the form of medicine which endeavours to cure diseases of the mind and problems of behaviour; and that *psychoanalysis* is a method of self-comprehension from which even the sanest human beings can benefit. The goal of *psychology* is to acquire understanding of behaviour and mental processes. The goal of *psychiatry* is allegedly to relieve mental and emotional distress and certainly to ensure that patients can cope with life and behave 'normally'; i.e. in a socially acceptable manner. The goal of *psychoanalysis* is to enable the patient to understand his or her own deepest motivations and thus function more effectively and with greater satisfaction in life.

As a result of his clinical work with patients during the latter years of the nineteenth century, Dr Sigmund Freud, a psychiatrist of Vienna, came to a conclusion that was then considered to be revolutionary: that our conscious mind is only a small part of our make-up and motivations, and that what really drive us are factors of which we are not usually aware, which reside in what he termed 'the unconscious'. To use the familiar analogy of an iceberg, the conscious mind is merely the visible tip. Fundamentally, Freud argued, we are driven by instincts identical with those of the animals and by far the most vital is sex. Freud termed this the *libido*.

Freud's contributions to human thought may be grouped under three headings – an instrument of research, the findings produced by the instrument and the theoretical hypotheses inferred from the findings. Although Freud originally employed hypnosis as his tool of research into the unconscious, he soon developed a new technique, that of 'free association'. In the words of James Strachey:

> He adopted the unheard-of plan of simply asking the person whose mind he was investigating to say whatever came into his head. This crucial decision led at once to the most startling results; even in this primitive form Freud's instrument produced fresh insight. For, though things went along swimmingly for a while, sooner or later the

flow of associations dried up: the subject would not or could not think of anything more to say. There thus came to light the fact of 'resistance', of a force, separate from the subject's conscious will, which was refusing to collaborate with the investigation. Here was one basis for a very fundamental piece of theory, for a hypothesis of the mind as something dynamic, as consisting in a number of mental forces, some conscious and some unconscious, operating now in harmony, now in opposition with one another.[1]

Secondly, Freud's own self-analysis led him to explore the nature of dreams. These he regarded as the expression of unconscious – and hence repressed – fears and yearnings. It is rather as though dreams are films made by a libertarian creator in a severely authoritarian society: he is not allowed to show his views plainly so he works in symbols. One of the tasks of the psychoanalyst is to interpret those symbols. Freud therefore evolved techniques of dream-analysis in order to penetrate the resistances of neurotic patients.

The popular press has made most people familiar with notions such as dreams of serpents being about the penis and hence displaying one's reaction to male sexuality. Unsurprisingly, given the nature of his time, this rather obvious equation was greeted with hysteria, hatred, ridicule and contempt when Freud first advanced it. Most people are familiar too with 'Freudian slips' – mistakes of speech which reveal an unconscious mental process – and platitudes such as: 'A man leaves his umbrella at a house to which he subconsciously wishes to return.' However, they may be relieved to learn that the founder of psychoanalysis possessed a sense of humour. At an international dinner of the world's leading psychoanalysts, Freud astounded and appalled the company by placing a huge cigar in his mouth and proceeding to smoke it with obvious relish. There were murmurs of consternation. 'This may be a phallus, gentlemen,' Freud admitted cheerfully, 'but let us not forget that it is also a cigar.'

Freud proceeded to develop hypotheses based upon the data elicited by his methods. Perhaps the best expression of his mature thoughts is *The Ego and the Id* (1923). Here Freud termed our uncoordinated instinctual desires the *id*. In society, these desires undergo a process of repression from the moment we are born. We are conditioned and suppressed by our parents, our schooling, our peers and the manners and customs of the society around us. This creates something within us which is often termed the conscience but which Freud termed the *superego*, the moralizing faculty. In most people, the superego and the id are continually in conflict. Moreover, we are creatures of conscious mentation and Freud termed this faculty the *ego*, which endeavours to mediate between superego and id. Freudian psychoanalysis aims to bring about insights into the experiences - usually stemming from childhood and long repressed and forgotten - which formed the id and the superego and into the customary processes of the ego. It is maintained that the resulting self-knowledge will liberate trapped energy and enable the patient to lead a much more fulfilling life.

Certain other concepts play a vital part in Freud's thought. He was the first to accept the facts of infantile sexuality; and there is the notion of the Oedipus complex. A complex can be defined as trapped energy; and/or as a problem which is not recognized or admitted by the conscious mind yet which nevertheless dictates thought, feeling and behaviour. Freudians argue that most men suffer from the Oedipus complex, which is the subconscious desire to imitate the example of Oedipus in Greek mythology: and kill one's father and fuck one's mother. These thoughts are so shocking, so forbidden, that they cannot be allowed to enter one's head. Consequently people do stupid things and feel terrible without knowing why, because they refuse to recognize their father-hatred and mother-lust. In common with Freud, Regardie came upon this phenomenon time and time again in his subsequent clinical experience; one result was his favourite joke:

Two Jewish women are walking along the street together and one says to the other: 'I have terrible news. My son – he's just been to the psychiatrist and the psychiatrist says he has an Oedipus complex.'

'*Ach*, Oedipus schmoedipus!' says the other. 'As long as he's a good Jewish boy and loves his mother.'

Freudian analysis, as most of its practitioners admit, is an inappropriate approach to the cure of *psychosis* – a disorder of the whole psyche usually classified as manic-depressive or as 'schizophrenia', a mysterious term which has yet to be clearly defined. However, the proponents of psychoanalysis argue that it can cure *neurosis* – an ailment of a psyche which is otherwise functioning more or less adequately. It purports to do this by bringing the patient to awareness of fears and desires which have hitherto not been allowed to surface into consciousness, turning the light of reason upon them and encouraging a healthy acceptance which drains away the psychic poison accumulated over the years, and liberates all the trapped energy. The process is not unlike a surgical operation whereby the surgeon uses his scalpel to cut through to the diseased organ, slices away the poisonous tissue and disinfects the wound, leaving the organ free to perform its proper function.

A classic neurosis, into which Regardie developed insights, is that of castration anxiety. This stems from the Oedipus complex. The man cannot and will not admit his subconscious desire to enjoy sexual congress with his mother. It is so dreadful a deed – as Freud aptly remarked in *Totem and Tabbo*: 'in the beginning was the deed' – arousing so much shame and guilt that the penalty must be equally atrocious. For this crime the man must lose his manhood and suffer castration. The resulting anxiety manifests in a variety of unrewarding behaviour patterns: impotence; inability to achieve sexual satisfaction; emotional and sexual division of women into 'pure' types like his fancy picture of his mother and with whom he cannot enjoy sexual relations – and 'whores' who are 'dirty' and 'disgusting', which all too familiar pattern is the insult to women of the inadequate male; a boring and unhealthy obsession with phallic symbols such as guns and sports cars; and above all, masochism.

By the end of his life, Regardie had treated innumerable masochists, as a result of which he was convinced that masochism stemmed directly from castration anxiety. In conversations with the present writer, he argued convincingly that the masochist is inwardly so terrified of castration for his repressed desire to make love to his mother, that he feels compelled – in order to avoid that dread – to undergo punishment and *symbolic* castration in various rituals of pain, shame, degradation and humiliation at the hands of a real or imagined mother-substitute.

Freud's outlook for humanity as expressed in a brilliant essay written when he was in his eighties, *Civilisation and Its Discontents*, was pessimistic. He had come to discern two contrary instincts struggling for control of the human psyche: *eros*, sex and life: and *thanatos*, death; and perhaps his experience of the Nazis had persuaded him that Thanatos would take charge within us. To a gentleman conditioned by the culture of late nineteenth-century Vienna, the full expression of the libido, though a vital matter for scientific investigation, was nevertheless profoundly disturbing. Freud thought that a measure of repression was a necessary and essential condition of human civilization. He advocated sublimation, the channelling of destructive impulses into consciously directed, socially beneficial and practically productive pursuits. Much as he admired the courage and insights of Freud, Regardie had certain doubts. He still pondered Crowley's view expressed in *Magick: In Theory and Practice*:

Professor Sigmund Freud and his school have, in recent years, discovered a part of this body of Truth, which has been taught for many centuries in the Sanctuaries of initiation. But failure to grasp the fullness of Truth, especially that implied in my Sixth Theorem ('Every man and every woman is a star') – and its corollaries, has led him and his followers into the error of admitting that the avowedly suicidal 'Censor' is the proper arbiter of conduct. Official psychoanalysis is therefore committed to upholding a fraud, although the foundation of the science was the observation of the disastrous effects on the individual of being false to his Unconscious Self, whose 'writing on the wall' in dream language is the record of the sum of the essential tendencies of the true nature of the individual. The result has been that psycho-analysts have misinterpreted life, and announced the absurdity that every human being is essentially an anti-social, criminal and insane animal. It is evident that the errors of the Unconscious of which the psycho-analysts complain are neither more nor less than the 'original sin' of the theologians whom they despise so heartily.

There was a further matter on which Regardie questioned Freud's wisdom: occultism. Occultism was one of the major issues which brought about the parting between Freud and his most promising student and colleague, Carl Gustav Jung (1875–1961) as perceptively related by the late James Webb:

The defection of Jung, the 'Crown Prince', Freud's favourite son, was a great blow to the founder of psycho-analysis but one of the strangest aspects of the relationship between Jung and Freud is that it occurred at all. Although Freud himself moved towards a consideration of the supernatural in the years 1921–2, it was with great reluctance and little skill, at least in taking the basic precautions against fraud ... At least up till the 1920's Freud maintained his distance from the occult, and on one occasion tried to make Jung promise to elevate his sexual theory of the neuroses into an unshakable bulwark 'against the black mud of occultism'. Jung in his turn thought that for Freud sex had become what he called a 'numenosum' – a sacred and absolute category. It has been said that Freud was afraid of religion and the occult: and that Jung was afraid of sex. Whatever the truth of this, Jung can be seen as the culminating point of the late 19th-century occult revival. He put into a terminology to which those brought up on the new and exciting language of Freud could respond, the insights into the psyche which the occultists and mystics of all ages had once expressed intelligibly – but which had been veiled and to all intents and purposes lost by the development of a vocabulary of modern science that excluded the areas of experience of which they spoke ...

. . .

A spectacular incident occurred in the presence of Freud himself. Jung visited his master in Vienna in 1909, and discussed Parapsychology with him. Freud denounced the whole area of inquiry in terms which annoyed Jung considerably, so much so that the Swiss psychologist felt his diaphragm becoming 'red-hot'. At that moment a loud explosion took place in a bookcase beside the two men. Jung told Freud that this was an 'example of so-called catalytic exteriorisation phenomena' and predicted a second explosion, which duly occurred. Freud was horrified, and initially tried to explain the incident away.[2]

Jung could not accept Freud's insistence on sex as being the root of one's deepest motivations, and finally broke with the former in 1913. Instead Jung came to posit the theory that we are driven by three primary instincts: the will to live; the will to create, or sex instinct; and the social or herd instinct. Subsequent research and reflection led him to add the religious instinct, unique to human beings, which urges one to seek transcendental meaning in the data presented by life.

Jung was responsible, too, for the concept of the *Collective Unconscious*. This is the notion that beneath the personal subconscious, there is an unconscious common to all. It is as old as humanity itself, it is all our collective needs, fears and desires, it inspires all true art, it is the realm of dreams and it is the repository of all the symbols of mankind.

The attentive reader may have noticed the similarity of this conception to the Magician's idea of the Astral, and the notion of 'scrying in the spirit vision'. Significantly, many contemporary Jungians use a technique whereby students and patients are encouraged to imagine a journey through a strange land – like a waking dream – and to heed the words of any 'guides' they encounter. This is a watered-down version of Golden Dawn technique for exploring the Astral or 'scrying' but it omits every safety precaution against self-deception and the eruption of self-destructive forces.

One can also discern parallels between Magic and analytical

psychology – as Jung termed his way – in the concept of *individuation*. He saw this as a journey of the self into the Unconscious, to bring its treasures back into consciousness. There were various stages on the way, as in Magic. According to Jung, first one encounters the 'shadow', all the violent aspects of the psyche which one has suppressed. In magical terms, this is the Dweller on the Threshold of Initiation; and it is the painful process of self-realization and self-acceptance which is all too likely to occur to an initiate of the GD Portal Grade. And, as in the GD Adeptus Minor initiation, the process moves on to the death of the illusory self and the resurrection of a deeper individuality.

The next stage is confrontation with the 'soul-image', the *anima* or *animus*: the feminine aspects of every man and the masculine aspects of every woman. After this, there follows the appearance within the psyche of *archetypes* – mythological figures recognized by all humanity. Men dream of 'the wise old man' and women of 'the great mother'. Jungians hold that this indicates healthy resolution of unconscious polarities. Finally, or so analytical psychologists intend, the individuated, fully integrated individual, who has examined, encountered, experienced and balanced all unconscious drives within the self, will go on his way rejoicing.

It is hardly surprising that Jung turned his attention to the occult. His *VII Sermones ad Mortues*, originally published anonymously, is heavily influenced by the Gnostics; his association with the Orientalist Richard Wilhelm led to a lifelong study of and reverence for the *I-Ching*; he was sufficiently impressed by Tibetan Tantra to write laudatory prefaces to the texts edited by Dr Evans-Wentz; he became engrossed in Alchemy, a subject to which we shall return in due course; and most important of all, he was affected throughout his life by psychic and mystical experiences. Nor is it at all astonishing that so many artists and occultists have been drawn to the work of Jung. Whereas for Freudians, the artist is all too often merely expressing his neuroses, for Jungians he is the High Priest of the Unconscious. This is equally true of the Magician: and no doubt both artist and Magician prefer the Jungian description of their activities to the Freudian. Occultists of the kind who neglect magical practice are furthermore delighted to find their dearest beliefs endorsed by so great a scientific and medical authority as Professor Jung.

Regardie soaked himself in Jung for a time but despite his respect for analytical psychology and his incorporation of many of its concepts into his own thought, he discerned certain objections. There is, for example, the question of will. Freud had seen will as a unity, a blind, thrusting force of instinct. Jung divided the will into four. It is easy to imagine a variety of circumstances in which the will to live, the sex instinct, the herd instinct and the religious instinct would be in conflict. How, and at what level of the Unconscious, is conflict between these inner, equally valid wills to be resolved? Is Jung maintaining that we are cursed with divided and on occasion mutually exclusive instincts from our very birth?

Again, it is difficult to be satisfied with his notion of the herd or social instinct as a primary drive. Some animals herd together: others don't. Humanity varies. The most important work in the advancement of human evolution has been done by men and women of solitary habits. What exactly *is* the herd or social instinct? Is it merely a natural blind need for company? Or is it that need for company which arises from deep insecurity? – in which case, it is surely a neurosis rather than an instinct. Or is it a desire to win approval in the eyes of others? – in which case the same comment applies. What can it have to do with individuation? The answers are best left to Jungians.

Secondly, Regardie was never satisfied with Jung's celebrated division of humankind into introverts and extraverts. For him, this was far too simplistic. His experience with patients clearly demonstrated that there are many individuals in whom introversion and extraversion co-exist. Thirdly, Regardie noticed a principal danger of analytical psychology and avoided it: the tendency to become trapped in a morass of symbolism and a maze of myth without ever getting to the point of the process. However, despite his objections to Jung and to Freud, he recognized the immense value of their work and it became a vital part of his thinking. One can clearly perceive the effects in his *The Art and Meaning of Magic*, (1970) a collection of three first-class essays written over the years. Therein one can find a lucid and rational exposition of Ceremonial Magic from a psychoanalytic perspective. This use of psychological terms in order to explain the subject reasonably was not entirely original. Back in the early 1900s, Crowley had endeavoured to equate Magic with cerebral neurology, thus making it a branch of science: in *The Initiated Interpretation of Ceremonial Magic*,[3] he argued that the spirits and demons evoked by the Magician are simply parts of the brain. Evocation is therefore a matter of stimulating chosen brain cells.

This physiological approach is limited by the substantial difficulties of devising appropriate experiments and was certainly handicapped by the lack of appropriate equipment in the early years of this century. By 1908, when he wrote *The Psychology of Hashish*, Crowley was advocating the method of psychological introspection and using Buddhist terms for the classification of states of consciousness; and he appealed to men of science to become pioneers in this field.

It was left to Regardie to employ the more elastic and popular terminology of psychoanalysis. In his essay, he stresses the essential sanity of Magic. Travel in the Astral? An exploration of the Unconscious. Divination? Awareness of the rhythms of the collective Unconscious. Evocation? The hallucination, through psycho-drama, of a complex, the energy of which is re-integrated into the psyche. Invocation? Contact with an archetype. Initiation? Individuation. In other words, Magic is a dynamic form of applied psychology. There are many who would subscribe to this eminently sane position and Regardie's arguments here are cogent and persuasive: but practitioners often find that this reductionism takes the magic out of Magic. Crowley recanted in 1909 and embraced the objectivist view: this position is simply that there is much more to reality than the physical universe of the materialist, that there is intelligent life in other dimensions, and that human beings can grow wiser and greater by means of their encounters with it. Regardie later modified his position too. The present writer recalls quoting the subjectivist position to Regardie in the latter's own written words. 'That was what I thought then,' he replied. 'I know better now.'

Five questions demanded Regardie's attention as a result of his plunge into psychoanalysis.

1 How could the disciplines of Magic and psychoanalysis (or analytical psychology) be brought together so as to be of further and lasting use to humankind? The goals were strikingly similar. Crowley had claimed that pschoanalysis was merely a branch, and a rotten branch at that, of Magick: Regardie was tempted to wonder whether Magic might be just a branch – albeit a very important one – of psychology.

2 Could magical and mystical illumination co-exist with neurosis? This problem vexed Regardie for years and will be discussed in due course. For him it was a crucial issue. If neurosis could co-exist with the highest illumination, then Magic alone wasn't enough. Psychoanalysis was perhaps an essential preliminary, even a necessary accompaniment. And if, on the other hand, neurosis and illumination were mutually exclusive, what on earth was one to make of Aleister Crowley?

3 Was the free association technique, consisting as it did of verbalization, sufficiently effective? We are all no doubt familiar with the sort of person who has psychoanalysis for ten years and praises the analyst as if Christ had returned to earth, yet the process doesn't seem to have done the blindest bit of good. One suspects that this is partly because times have changed so drastically since Freud first expounded his theories. In the Vienna of the 1890s, Freud's ideas had had a galvanizing effect upon the psyche which they do not have today, when familiarity has dulled us. The statement 'This reveals that secretly you wish to kill your father and rape your mother' could then have had the same shock effect as

the sudden utterance of a Zen Master, which instantly induces enlightenment in the student. Today we have an obvious defence mechanism in intellectualization. It is easy to imagine an intelligent patient calmly stating to the analyst: 'Yes, you're quite right. No doubt there is within me a secret but desperate desire to kill my father and rape my mother. All right, I know that now. But how is this knowledge of the slightest assistance to me?' Considerations of this nature led Regardie to examine the work of those who were pioneering alternative, non-intellectual, non-verbal therapies, most notably Wilhelm Reich, to whom we shall be returning.

4 Magic and psychoanalysis were both processes of 'Know Thyself' and 'Be Thyself'; of making the vast resources of the Unconscious conscious: how, then, could they be advantageously combined so as to bring an ordinary individual to consciousness of his or her own innate divinity? How, in fact, could these disciplines be used specifically to aid Israel Regardie?

5 Was Freud right in asserting that our primary drive is sex? If so – and here Regardie came to reject the complexities of Jung and embrace the simplicity of Freud – to what extent was an element of social repression necessary if civilization were to flourish?

Regardie's later involvement with the work of Reich would clarify the matter. In the meantime, he considered the Freudian view of religion – most ably set forth by Freud in *The Future of an Illusion* – that God was merely another name for the sex instinct: and contrasted it with Crowley's point that: 'When you have proved that God is merely a name for the sex instinct, it appears to me not far to the perception that the sex instinct is God.'

Notes

1 James Strachey, 'Sigmund Freud: A Sketch of his Life and Ideas', *Sigmund Freud. 2. New Introductory Lectures on Psychoanalysis*, Pelican.

[2] James Webb, 'Carl Jung, in (ed.) *The Encyclopedia of the Unexplained.*
[3] '*The Initiated Interpretation of Ceremonial Magic*' can be found in the Notes to *The Sword of Song* in *The Collected Works of Aleister Crowley*, Vol. II (1905–7); and in Crowley's Preface to his edition of *Goetia*, (1905).

8

A Friend in Jesus?

It is said by the Alchemists that prior to the appearance of the Philosopher's Stone they seek and the interior ecstasy which is the accompaniment of its appearance, there is a stage of putrefaction. The Magician sees the matter in similar terms and expresses it in the formula IAO. As Crowley has it:

> *In beginning a meditation practice, there is always a quiet pleasure*, a gentle natural growth; one takes a lively interest in the work; it seems easy; one is quite pleased to have started. This stage represents Isis. Sooner or later *it is succeeded by depression* – the Dark Night of the Soul, an infinite weariness and detestation of the work. The simplest and easiest acts become almost impossible to perform. Such impotence fills the mind with apprehension and despair. The intensity of this loathing can hardly be understood by any person who has not experienced it. This is the period of Apophis.
>
> It is followed by the arising not of Isis, but of Osiris. *The ancient condition is not restored, but a new and superior condition is created*, a condition only rendered possible by the process of death ...
>
> Even in the legend of Prometheus we find an identical formula concealed; and a similar remark applies to those of Jesus Christ, and of many other mythical god-men worshipped in different countries.[1]

IAO is in this context the formula of elementary mysticism in all its branches.

Psychoanalysts are familiar with the phenomena which occur when a patient becomes conscious of the conflicting drives within the psyche, the resulting anxiety, and the need for security which is usually fixated upon the analyst and called *transference*. In any event the fact remains that Regardie passed through a curious stage of Christian mysticism.

A variety of factors moved him to investigate the subject. He wanted to familiarize himself with all methods of mystical attainment. Mysticism is the transcending of intellectual boundaries in a union with the Infinite. It is argued by mystics that if rational thought is pursued far enough, it ends in self-contradiction. A similar conclusion can be reached by the successive study of Berkeley, Hume and Kant in the Western philosophical tradition. In other words, we cannot apprehend ultimate truth about the Infinite by the use of the finite intellect. We will have to use methods of unleashing other faculties of the brain.

All statements concerning Mysticism – other than denials of its validity – fall into two categories: the prescriptive and the descriptive. Prescriptive statements recommend or exhort courses of action; they say: 'Do x.' Descriptive statements expound the experience of the subject. They might be highly specific: e.g. 'I saw a red rose, heard a bell chime once, smelled burning wood and felt a piercing pain in my heart.' Or they might be vague and woolly: e.g. 'I was bathed in a vibrating ocean of God's love.' Unfortunately, the statements of too many mystics are of the latter variety. It is very hard to express the inexpressible, to translate what is beyond reason into the words of reason. It is like describing sight to one born blind or orgasm to a six year old. Many mystics lack literary ability – there is no reason why they should have it – and this makes the task even more difficult than it already is.

In the words of the Hindu proverb, Regardie panted after God as a miser after gold. He did indeed at times experience deep and glowing interior illumination: he built his life on these experiences: but he could not express them. In common with many, he had to turn to art and poetry in which others expressed what he felt so deeply. This was why Crowley was his favourite author, why he memorized certain mystical passages, why he was so fond of quoting favourite pieces in his books as recommended prayers. One passage in particular describes Regardie's state at this period.

> Weary, weary! saith the scribe. Who shall lead me to the sight of Rapture of my master?

The body is weary and the soul is sore weary and sleep weighs down their eyelids; yet ever abides the sure consciousness of ecstasy, unknown, yet known in that its being is certain. O Lord, be my helper, and bring me to the bliss of the Beloved.[2]

Regardie had thrown himself into Hindu, Buddhist and Jewish Mysticism. Now he tried the Christian version. It was another gesture of independence from Crowley, who openly despised every manifestation of the Christian religion. However, even Crowley had recommended the *Spiritual Exercises* of Ignatius Loyola as first-class Yoga; and Regardie had quoted and praised the work in *The Tree of Life*. Christianity has further advantages. There is much safety and comfort in the faith for anyone tormented by shame, fear and guilt which, as Regardie openly admitted years later, was still his inner state of being at that time.

The essence of the Christian religion is really quite simple.[3] It is held that God so loved the world despite its wickedness that He sent His only begotten Son, Jesus Christ, to redeem it. After a short but remarkable life packed with incident, teachings, parables, prophecy and even miracles, the Son of God was arrested and tried by the authorities, then crucified publicly between two thieves. It is believed that despite his death and entombment, Jesus imitated the legends of Adonis, Attis, Osiris and Dionysus and rose from the dead then ascended bodily into heaven. It is stated that Jesus is the intermediary between humankind and God, that He will judge us after our deaths and that no man cometh to the Father save by Him. For, it is insisted, in dying in agony on the Cross, Jesus Christ atoned for and redeemed all the sins of humanity, past, present and future. If we are Christians, our primary task is to have faith in the above propositions; many Protestant sects hold that faith alone can save us from the fires of Hell, a place of everlasting torment to which the unbelievers are sent along with the wicked. Provided that our faith is sufficiently strong, Christ will forgive us all our sins and when we die, we will be granted eternal bliss in the presence of Jesus. Roman Catholics agree that faith is essential but hold that works are required too. A good Catholic must keep the commandments of Christ and obey the Church if everlasting damnation in Hell is to be avoided.

Compared to Hinduism, Buddhism or even Judaism, Christianity must seem somewhat unsophisticated intellectually to any unprejudiced observer, yet it has enjoyed and still enjoys extraordinary appeal. This is partly on account of its simplicity. All one has to do is worship Jesus, believe in the *Bible* – and, if a Catholic, in the words of the Pope, priests and nuns – try to obey Christ's teachings and ask for forgiveness every time one sins against them. Its appeal to the guilt-ridden is obvious. One simply submits to Jesus and gets loved in return. This is the ultimate attraction. It doesn't matter how vile you are: *Jesus loves you*!

The attentive reader may have noticed a mild antipathy to the Christian faith on the part of the present writer: for his part, he does not enjoy contemplating the idea of the six million human beings who were tortured and murdered as 'witches' and heretics between the fifteenth and seventeenth centuries by sincere and devout Christians.[4] Nevertheless one must ask which factors within Christianity fascinated Regardie. Perhaps the most significant was the notion of Divine Love.

It is said that 'Perfect Love casteth out all Fear' – and Regardie was attracted by a Catholic saint who is often celebrated as an example of Perfect Love: St Francis of Assisi. Regardie delighted in the saint's worship of Nature and of all living creatures; he shared it; and at times the resemblance became so marked that an older woman with whom he was having a love-affair named him 'Francis'. After that and for the rest of his life, his friends would call him Francis. The lady in question had a profound effect upon her lover. By his own verbal account, she was the second of three women who brought him through a vital stage of self-realization – the first was Maria Teresa de Miramar. In old age he would strongly advise young men to have at least one affair with a woman old enough to be one's mother; 'Gets all the Oedipal shit out of you.'[5]

Of particular interest to Regardie was the notion that the Power of Jesus Christ could heal mortal affliction. This led him to a study of New Thought and Christian Science. New Thought derived from the theories of P. D. Quimby (1802–66) who believed that physical diseases were produced by wrong ideas and attitudes and that patients could be cured by changing their beliefs. The guiding principle of New Thought is 'as a man thinks, so he is' and it uses the power of positive thinking to heal disease. The International New Thought Alliance has summarized its goals:

> To teach the Infinitude of the Supreme One: the Divinity of man and his infinite possibilities through the creative power of constructive thinking and obedience to the voice of the indwelling Presence, which is our source of Inspiration, Power, Health and Prosperity.

Quimby greatly influenced Mary Baker Eddy (1821–1910) who founded the Church of Christian Science to teach that sin, disease, death and matter itself are illusions, based on man's failure to comprehend his true, godlike nature. Its method of healing, therefore, is to dispense with medicine, to dismiss illness as error caused by misunderstanding, and to rely on a true love and acceptance of God. Even in his seventies, Regardie defended Mrs Eddy.

> One of my friends of many years ago, the late Dr Hereward Carrington complained that I was leaning over backwards in my attempt to be fair to Mrs Eddy. If this is in fact the case, then I must confess to a profound respect for this really extraordinary woman. Insofar as she was constantly ill and a self-confessed failure through to her sixtieth year, it seems a remarkable achievement to have completely turned around the direction of her spiritual energies for creative ends during the remaining years of her life. There are not many people of whom this can be said. The average person is fairly well played out by sixty. The fires of life are beginning to dim, if not

go out altogether. She is thus worthy of detailed study and attention (Foreword to *The Teachers of Fulfillment*).

Nevertheless, Regardie could not restrain his persistently questing intelligence. This led him to reject the historical foundations of Christianity and ultimately to concur with Crowley.

'Jesus' is a composite figure of several incompatible elements. There is therefore no 'he' in the case. The Gospels are a crude compilation of Gnosticism, Judaism, Essenism, Hinduism, Buddhism, with the watch-words of various sacerdotal–political cults, thrown at random into a hotch-potch of distorted legends of the persons of the Pagan Pantheon, and glued with a semblance of unity in the interests of sustaining the shaken fabric of local faiths against the assaults of the consolidation of civilisation, and of applying the cooperative principle to businesses whose throats were being cut by competition (*Crowley on Christ*).

As Regardie said soberly to me on Good Friday, 1982; 'Jesus Christ never existed. It's all a bunch of legends of the time cobbled together in an unsatisfactory formula of Osiris.' Even so, he still believed that there are elements in New Thought and Christian Science from which one could profitably learn. It could not be denied that in many cases, the techniques of healing worked. Then perhaps one could postulate the existence of some great, cosmic, Godlike force which could heal and transform and which was non-sectarian.

Regardie would express his comprehension of the Christian Science and New Thought perspectives in 1946 with *The Romance of Metaphysics*, subsequently republished as *The Teachers of Fulfillment*. It was based on studies of ten years before and bears the following dedication: 'CLARE, dear friend, this book is dedicated to you, with fond and grateful memories of the early thirties.' In the opinion of the present writer, this is the least interesting and least lively of all Regardie's works. However, one can certainly respect the motives which impelled its creation: a need to earth all that had been learned in the form of a printed book: and a desire to expound metaphysical methods of healing. Additionally, Regardie had observed that effective psychotherapy brings out a confused hunger for metaphysics in the patient and he therefore wanted to point out elementary approaches in plain language. His concern, strongly influenced by his studies in psychology, was increasingly the here and now. Some advocated seeking the Light up in Heaven: Regardie, like a Prometheus of the spirit, sought after ways of bringing Light down to Earth.

The Teachers of Fulfillment is a long, detailed and intelligent study of Christian Science, New Thought and the Unity School of Christianity, whose doctrines are an amalgam of the two. To my knowledge, it remains the standard text on the subject. The second edition (1983) boasts a Preface by Bhagavan Jivananda and an Introduction by Colin Wilson who concludes: 'It is this insight which pervades this remarkable book on metaphysics, and which makes it, to me, the most personal and moving of all Regardie's works.' Unfortunately, Colin Wilson's Introduction to Regardie's *Energy, Prayer and Relaxation* also concludes: 'It is this insight that pervades this little book on energy, relaxation and prayer, and which makes it, to me, the most personal and moving of all Regardie's writings.'

Perhaps the confusion arose because *Energy, Prayer and Relaxation* (1982) was originally part – the last three chapters – of *The Romance of Metaphysics*, now republished without that section as *The Teachers of Fulfillment*. *Energy, Prayer and Relaxation* is remarkably good and in due course we shall set forth its concerns: for the present, our concern is why Regardie chose to separate it from the original. This was in the main because his approach to Christianity had altered. *The Teachers of Fulfillment* ends with Regardie exhorting the reader to pray with the words: *The forgiving love of Jesus Christ is expressed in me*. By the 1980s, he had developed a deep dislike of Christianity and was editing and introducing Crowley's vitriolic diatribe against the religion, *The World's Tragedy*. Furthermore, although he had a low opinion of Anton LaVey's Church of Satan, he held that it was healthier to go there than to the Church of Christ. He had been lured to Christianity by its promise of the forgiving love of Jesus for every weakness. It was fortunate for him that he perceived his blunder and repudiated such faith as he may have temporarily acquired. Yet the experience wouldn't be wasted. Regardie asked himself why it was necessary to have the Christian in the Science.

The theory of this Science is that there is some force pervading all life in the Universe which can heal and harmonize mind and body.

Regardie craved for that healing and harmony. During his years in England, 1929–37, his life was continually uncertain, complicated and stressful. He suffered from constant poverty. Snobs looked down on him: when Crowley had sent him to his Jermyn Street tailors, the assistants ushered him downstairs to the servants' and chauffeurs' section – an insult he never forgot. His books brought him very little money and it was a continuous struggle to write them. Freudian analysis was doing nothing for his asthma.

To repeat his question: 'Why're Magicians always so poor? You never meet a poor Christian Scientist.' Regardie wanted to isolate the techniques from their Christian context. Surely what was wanted was simply something that worked for ordinary people?

In the course of his research, it was inevitable that Regardie would tackle a horribly difficult subject which nevertheless promises divine transmutation of the being.

Alchemy.

Notes

1 Crowley, *Magick: In Theory and Practice*. There are more profound considerations involving the formula of IAO but they lie beyond the scope of this work.

[2] Crowley, *The Book of the Heart Girt with a Serpent*, also known as *Liber LXV*, published in *The Holy Books of Thelema*.

[3] For the record, the present writer was baptized into the Church of England and largely educated at Church of England foundations but was never confirmed in the Christian faith.

[4] For a detailed exposition of this sickening matter, see Russell Hope Robbins, FRCL, *An Encyclopedia of Witchcraft and Demonology*.

[5] I later took Regardie's advice and was delighted with the results.

9

Solve et Coagula

Let it suffice to say that the word alchemy is an Arabic term consisting of the article 'al' and the adjective 'kehmi' which means 'that which pertains to Egypt'. A rough translation would be 'The Egyptian matter'. The assumption is what the Mohammedan grammarians held traditionally, that the art was derived from that wisdom of the Egyptians which was the boast of Moses, Plato, and Pythagoras, and the source of their illumination.

Modern research (by profane scholars) leaves it still doubtful as to whether Alchemical treatises should be classified as mystical, magical, medical, or chemical. The most reasonable opinion is that all these objects formed the pre-occupation of the alchemists in varying proportions (Crowley: *Magick: In Theory and Practice*).

The word is usually understood by the layman as the endeavour to transmute base metals into gold. Although historians of science have dismissed this endeavour as ignorant and silly, they nevertheless have credited the medieval alchemists and their successors as the founders, through their experimental work, of modern chemistry. Further enquiry elicits the information that the alchemists were in fact seeking some substance which would accomplish the transmutation of metals, which they called the Philosopher's Stone. This was also the Stone of the Wise and the Medicine of Metals: from it one could easily make the Elixir of Life which cures all diseases and confers immortality. If the alchemist succeeded in his quest, therefore, he enjoyed health and wealth in abundance and forever.

Many alchemists wrote extraordinary books, usually excruciatingly obscure, containing equally extraordinary illustrations teeming with bizarre and beautiful symbols. These treatises make it obvious that the alchemists were not benighted fools chasing health and wealth through some lunatic notions of Chemistry. Certainly there were those who imitated them without any comprehension – the *souffleurs*, the charlatans and the cranks – and these brought upon Alchemy the scorn bitingly expressed, for instance, in Chaucer's *The Canon's Yeoman's Prologue* and Jonson's *The Alchemist*. However, one cannot airily dismiss a subject whose exponents included Roger Bacon, Albertus Magnus, Nicolas Flamel, Basil Valentinus, Paracelsus, John Dee or Van Helmont. Essentially, the true alchemists were mystics. What they sought was the blaze of the divine light within the interior spirit, of which the appearance of the Philosopher's Stone was but the outward sign of inner grace. The true alchemists were Magicians also. As Crowley observed, alchemical texts

> all begin with a substance in nature which is described as existing almost everywhere, and as universally esteemed of no value. The alchemist is in all cases to take this substance, and subject it to a series of operations. By so doing, he obtains his product. This product, however named or described, is always a substance which represents the truth or perfection of the original 'First Matter'; and its qualities are invariably such as pertain to a living being, not to an inanimate mass. In a word, the alchemist is to take a dead thing, impure, valueless, and powerless, and transform it into a live thing, active, invaluable and thaumaturgic ... The First Matter is a man, that is to say, a perishable parasite, bred of the earth's crust, crawling irritably upon it for a span, and at last returning to the dirt whence he sprang. The process of initiation consists in removing his impurities, and finding in his true self an immortal intelligence to whom matter is no more than the means of manifestation.[1]

Very few realized these relatively simple points and alchemists were generally dismissed as imbeciles until 1850 when Mary Anne Attwood published *A Suggestive Enquiry into the Hermetic Mystery*, in which she argued that the true goal of Alchemy was spiritual perfection. This marked the commencement of deeper understanding. In the twentieth century, Carl Jung turned his finest attention to the matter.

Jung noticed alchemical symbolism cropping up in the dreams of patients who knew nothing whatever of alchemy. He believed that these symbols came from the 'collective unconscious' and regarded the alchemical work as a process of 'individuation', the development of an integrated personality. The various stages, trials and difficulties of the work were a projection of the long, toilsome path towards unity of the self.[2]

In *Psychology and Alchemy* (1953) Jung concluded that Alchemy was 'rather like an undercurrent to the Christianity that ruled on the surface'. He used the alchemical process as a model for the progress of the patient.

Regardie's early views on Alchemy were taken from Crowley, especially the idea that the correct interpretation of Alchemy is in fact sexual. Many texts do bear this interpretation and make absolute sense when viewed in terms of Sex Magick: this point has been made convincingly by Regardie in *The Tree of Life*, where technical Sex Magick is described in vivid alchemical terms as the Mass of the Holy Ghost; and in cruder and plainer fashion by Louis T. Culling in *A Manual of Sex Magick*. The question remains as to whether the sexual interpretation is the only valid one. Regardie came to think not. He was persuaded to an alternative interpretation by his study of Jung and was galvanized into writing another book by his scrutiny of Attwood's work. This book was *The Philosopher's Stone*, a commentary on three alchemical texts from the perspective of Attwood and Jung.

Some sort of key is definitely needed if there is to be any comprehension of alchemical texts. For instance, the Philosopher's Stone itself, the ultimate goal of the Great Work, is never clearly defined. It exists everywhere in nature – yet it is ignored or despised. It is unknown – but everybody knows about it. It is made of fire – and water. It is a fluid – but it weighs nothing. It comes from God – except that it doesn't. Alchemists are also unhelpful in their descriptions of the processes by which one may achieve it. The language of the alchemist's art is one of symbol.

The king and queen, the serpent devouring its own tail, the phoenix, the dragon, the peacock's tail, the tree, the bath, the mountain, the rose, the green lion, the unicorn, the crucified snake, virgin's milk, the massacre of the innocents and innumerable other emblems make up the symbolic language of the art.[3]

Nevertheless, Richard Cavendish has managed to make some sense out of the subject:

It remained a cardinal principle of alchemy that you could reduce a metal or other material (and yourself psychologically and spiritually) to first matter by stripping all its characteristics from it. This was to 'kill' it. You could then restore it to 'life' and add desirable characteristics to it, or 'nurture' it like a growing child, until it became the Stone. The 'death' of the material is the mock death of initiation into the Mysteries, and of initiation rituals in many societies, which is followed by 'rebirth' to a new and better life. The whole secret of the art was said to be contained in the maxim *Solve et coagula*, 'Dissolve and combine'. To 'dissolve' means to strip away a substance's characteristics, to 'combine' is to build up a new substance.

Moreover:

The first steps in the work, leading up to the process called 'putrefaction' culminated in the *nigredo*, or black stage, when the material in the alchemist's vessel had been reduced to first matter and its innate spark of life had been driven out of it in the form of vapour. This was called the Black Crow, Black Sun or Raven's Head, and might be represented by a dead and rotting corpse, a black bird, or a dead king eaten by a wolf. After this the 'dead' material was 'reborn' as its own vapour condensed into a liquid and saturated it, and this was soon followed by the *albedo*, or whitening, when the white tincture or white elixir formed in the vessel. The final processes led on to the *rubedo*, the appearance of the red tincture, red elixir or red powder, the miraculous Stone itself.

The alchemist laboured over his furnace and crucible, repeating the same operations over and over again, reading and re-reading his authorities and struggling to make sense of them, patiently wrestling with inefficient equipment and incompetent or dishonest assistants, surviving explosions, catastrophes and disappointments, devoutly praying for help from on high. And eventually, perhaps, the illumination would come, the great secret he had toiled and suffered for so long would dawn on his mind. Often, the alchemists said, the secret would be revealed by a figure in a dream, an angel or an old, wise man. It has been suggested, tentatively, that on rare occasions alchemists may have succeeded in making gold, if only in tiny quantities, through a type of Psychokinesis, the influence of the mind on matter.[5]

At the time of writing *The Philosopher's Stone*, however, Regardie would not have agreed with the view of Cavendish that Alchemy was an actual physical process of metallurgy. He had fallen into the classic Jungian trap whereby nothing is real and everything is a symbol of some other symbol. In consequence, Regardie dismisses the chemical content of Alchemy and translates everything into the language of analytical psychology and generalized spiritual development. The book is unquestionably interesting reading but the present writer must forbear from further comment at his late subject's explicit request. 'By far my worst book,' he added. 'Wish I'd never written it.'

It says much for Regardie's integrity that when *The Philosopher's Stone* was republished in the 1970s, he wrote a new Introduction in which he publicly recanted his earlier views. Contact with 'Frater Albertus' of the Paracelsus Research Society, Salt Lake City, Utah, had revolutionized his perspective. This society issues 'alchemical laboratory bullet-ins' and appears to proceed in accordance with a work called *The Alchemist's Handbook*. According to Francis King and Isabel Sutherland:

> The *Alchemists' Handbook*, written by 'Frater Albertus', who would seem to be the presiding genius of the Paracelsus Research Society, is largely concerned with the production of herbal elixirs by alchemical means. It is clear, however, that Frater Albertus has carried out a great deal of experimentation on metals and minerals.

For in an appendix to the *Handbook* he refers to such personal achievements as the preparation of vinegar of antimony 'according to the formula of Valentine' and the manufacture of the 'essences' of lead, copper, and gold.[6]

As a result of the sharing of information and practical laboratory experimentation, Regardie grew convinced that Alchemy began, continued and ended in working with physical substances; that this was indeed a valid if difficult way of realizing the divine self by changing the human self; and that anyone with sufficient determination, dedication and persistence could attempt it. He set up his own small laboratory and went to work. One experiment in quest of the Elixir of Life went disastrously wrong and an explosion affected his lungs, giving him the dyspnoea from which he ever afterwards suffered intermittently. The results of his other experiments are not known.

The pursuits of the alchemists should not be lightly dismissed. Even if the Philosopher's Stone appears only rarely, there are other notable benefits. Operations of Alchemy have erupted in discoveries vital to chemistry and medicine in the past – one thinks of Paracelsus' discoveries of opium, zinc and hydrogen, for instance – and may do so again in the future. The goals of Alchemy and the self-discipline and total absorption demanded by the art put it on the same exalted level as Yoga and Magic. Perhaps previous textual commentators have been mistaken in their endeavour to translate Alchemy into another and probably more limited language. In so doing, possibly we rob ourselves of a potential benefit. The beauty which abides in alchemical treatises derives surely from the apt choices of symbol and phrase, glyph and word, for the description of interior mystical experience and the accompanying processes of the physical world.

Unfortunately, the alchemists make sense – and good sense – only to alchemists, and others who endeavour to transmute their gross being into something finer and nobler; and who are thus familiar with altered states of consciousness. They make no sense at all to anybody else, save possibly students of quantum physics, nuclear energy and polarized light.

There is one obvious objection to Alchemy. Though its benefits – especially its ultimate material rewards – are obvious, it does appear to be the most difficult, complex and obscure method for transmutation of the being. Its proponents would no doubt argue that it has the advantage from the start of involving the physical world and the body in addition to the imagination, intellect, emotions and spirit, with results perpetually evident in the behaviour of metals and herbs within the vessel above the furnace. Clearly, Alchemy is a valid, time-honoured way to the divine which may also possess the potential for future discoveries of benefit to mankind, and some will always be drawn to 'the Art which requires the whole man'.

Sensing that a major European war was imminent, Regardie left England in 1937. He was glad to go back to America after nine hectic, strenuous, traumatic and yet rewardingly productive years. As he stated in *The Eye in the Triangle*:

> After my experience with the Golden Dawn and a lengthy Freudian analysis, for both of which I can say in all humility and simplicity – thank God! – I returned home to the United States. It was with a sigh of relief as I sailed into New York harbour, after the wild storms and turmoils of the preceding hectic years, years of initiation, harassment and, I hope, growth. It was good to leave the areas where conflict had become accentuated.

Yes, he had experienced and would continue to experience the *Solve* – but where was the *Coagula*?

Notes

1 Crowley, *Magick: In Theory and Practice.*
2 Richard Cavendish, 'Alchemy' in *The Encyclopedia of the Unexplained.*
3 Ibid.
4 Ibid.

[5] Ibid.
[6] Francis King and Isabel Sutherland, *The Rebirth of Magic* (1972).

10

The Art of True Healing

On his arrival in America, Regardie threw himself into psychotherapy and the work of Wilhelm Reich. The next ten years were as demanding in their way as the preceding decade. He took a degree in psychology from the Chiropractic College of New York city, graduating in 1941; as we know, he quarrelled violently with Crowley and repudiated his memory; he joined the US Army, 1942–5 – a step he later called 'a ghastly error. We were so inefficient, I don't know how we won the war. I can only assume that the enemy was even more inefficient': he studied psychotherapy with Dr Nandor Fodor; after the war he obtained a doctorate in psychology; and he moved to Los Angeles in 1947, where he set up a practice as a state-licensed chiropracter and, for those who indicated interest, a psychotherapist and healer. In time he would also teach psychiatry at the Los Angeles College of Chiropractic and contribute essays to *Psychiatric Quarterly* and *The American Journal of Psychotherapy*.

In later life he repeatedly emphasized that Magic *and* psychotherapy 'changed the course of my whole life'. How come? What was it about the work of Wilhelm Reich which had so deep and moving an effect upon Regardie? Why did the United States government authorities imprison Reich and seize and burn his books and manuscripts? What did the man have to say that was so terrible?

Wilhelm Reich (1897–1957) was born in Austro-Hungary and qualified as a physician in 1922. There followed two years of postgraduate neurological work under Professor Wagner-Jauregg. Although Wagner-Jauregg was a bitter foe of psychoanalysis, Reich nevertheless became a full member of the Vienna Psychoanalytic Society and practised Freudian analysis. Gradually he came to the conclusion that sexuality was the 'centre around which revolves the whole of social life as well as the inner life of the individual'.

Two concepts are vital to Reich's thought. One is that of *physiological armouring*, that physical symptoms without any neurological cause are the result of the body adopting a posture, gesture or appearance designed to communicate an inner, psychological happening. The second is his perception of schizophrenia as a 'bottling up' of energy in the autonomic nervous system. The evolution of his thought has been adroitly described by Francis King:

> Reich's idea was that psychic disturbances cause muscular tension, that this tension (armouring) reinforces the original psychic upheaval and that, by a dialectical interaction between mind and muscle, a self-perpetuating process of progressive physical and psychological degeneration is established. Reich believed that this process could only be reversed by a therapy designed to treat both mind and body. The first was to be tackled by fairly orthodox psychoanalytic treatment, the second by deep massage and physical manipulations designed to break up muscular armouring. Reich called the latter process *vegetotherapy* because he believed that the energy prevented from being released by armouring was stored up in the autonomic (or vegetative) nervous system. It must be emphasized that Reich was not so physiologically illiterate (as some Freudians have suggested) as to believe that the muscles are part of the autonomic system![1]

Throughout his life he was a champion of sexual freedom, and Communists and Nazis came to abhor him. Scientists usually deride Reich's later work on 'orgone energy'. For he came to believe, as a result of his experiments, that *orgone* was the basic life-stuff of the Universe, pervading all living things. *Vegetotherapy* therefore became a process of liberating the orgone energy within a human being, enabling it to flow and pulse freely. Reich also developed a large upright box, big enough for a man to sit in, called an 'orgone energy accumulator': he believed that this accumulator could extract orgone energy from the atmosphere and radiate it into the human body so as to cure every variety of physical and mental illness. Francis King relates the sad ending:

By this time Reich had settled in the United States, and he soon became engaged in the sale of his books and orgone devices through the mails. This attracted the attention of the US Food and Drug Administration, which decided that orgone energy did not exist and that Reich's accumulators were fraudulent devices; and, in 1950, obtained an injunction forbidding their distribution. Reich disregarded this injunction - he did not believe that any court had the right to adjudicate on a matter of scientific theory. He was sent to prison for contempt of court and died there in November 1957.[2]

Reich was a victim of what he himself had termed the *emotional plague*. As Regardie states in *The Eye in the Triangle*:

'The term "emotional plague" has no defamatory connotation.' This is Wilhelm Reich's definition. It does not refer to conscious malice, moral or biological degeneration, immorality, etc., but a person who, from birth, is constantly impeded in his natural way of living and so *develops artificial forms of locomotion*. He limps or moves on crutches, as it were. Similarly, an individual moves through life by means of the emotional plague if, from birth, his natural, self-regulatory instincts have been suppressed. The individual afflicted with the emotional plague limps *characterologically speaking*. The emotional plague may be considered a chronic biopathy of the organism. It is an epidemic disease, like schizophrenia or cancer, manifesting itself essentially in *Social living*. Schizophrenia and cancer are biopathies resulting from the plague in social life, whose effects are to be seen in the organism as in social living. Periodically, like any other plague, it takes on the dimensions of a pandemic, in the form of a gigantic break-through of sadism and criminality, as for example in the Catholic inquisition of the middle ages or the international fascism of the present century.

It was the emotional plague which caused Reich's enemies to persecute the man and burn his books for, as Regardie states:

People who employ such a compulsive morality are actually terrified

> at the emotional and instinctual possibilities latent within them. Unconsciously, they have imprisoned themselves in a meshwork of highly complex defense-mechanisms which block all possibility of spontaneous behaviour. This network functions as an armor, both on the psychological level as inhibitions, and on the somatic level as muscular tensions and visceral dysfunctions. Anyone who is capable of operating relatively freely, without the intervention of the armor, would awaken their hostility and resentment. Such a person would represent all that they have hated and feared. He would be a threat which could undo all they have managed through a lifetime to repress (*The Eye in the Triangle*).

To return to basics: *psychotherapy* means simply the healing of the psyche. The phrase is used as an umbrella to cover all methods which are not Freudian, Jungian, Adlerian or Gestalt. A principal way is that of Reich. His therapy is primarily non-verbal. This short-circuits all verbal defence-mechanisms. The therapist uses varieties of massage and physical manipulation while the patient is often instructed to hyperventilate, a practice not dissimilar to certain forms of Pranayama in Yoga. The intention is to break down the character armour, the front of false selfhood which we put up to other people and to ourselves in a continual denial of all we really feel. The goal of the therapist is for the patient to achieve union with the throbbing, pulsating, healing force of life itself which permeates every cell. We block off from that union on account of the pain and repression we have experienced. We forbid the admission and expression of that pain. Unconsciously we plaster anger all over our pain then, since the expression of anger is often considered to be socially unacceptable, we don't even admit to that anger and so degenerate into mean-spirited creatures who waste yet more energy in pretending to be 'nice' and consequently hate themselves for the emotional dishonesty and frustration involved. This deeply unsatisfactory process gives one rigid character armour – a limiting, restricting and regrettable acquisition. It is expressed in an unconscious cramping of the muscles and blockages within the autonomic nervous system. This is why Reichian psychotherapy goes directly to the body. The object is to dissolve the neuro-musculature armouring which divorces outer ego from inner life.

The process is painful. The massage itself hurts. The therapist works especially on deeply sensitive areas – the mouth, the throat, the solar plexus and the abdomen. These, perhaps unsurprisingly, equate roughly with positions of endocrine glands, the *chakras* of Yoga and the middle pillar of the kabbalistic Tree of Life, when visualised upon the human body. There are innumerable case histories of the results.

For instance, the patient may find that as her mouth is being massaged, she suddenly recalls a dog she'd entirely forgotten but which she'd loved with all her heart at the age of four. She suddenly remembers that one day, the dog was run over by a car. She wanted so much to cry for the sadness and grief of it but her parents always told her to shut up whenever she cried or else laughed at her and told her that tears were only for cissies. Literally, she bit back the tears. A neuro-muscular cramp around her mouth resulted. When the psychotherapist dissolves that cramp, she will cry her eyes out, sob her heart out and release all the trapped energy which was curdling within, poisoning her psyche and preventing her true fulfilment. When her solar plexus is tackled, she will scream out everything she ever wanted to scream but had to suppress: and Reichian massage of the abdomen customarily elicits uncontrollable writhing of the belly, accompanied by a vivid and virulent verbal torrent of obscenity.

In their journeys to wholeness, adventurers of the psyche shriek, yell, howl, bellow, vomit and faint. Afterwards they speak of the great inner peace which follows, of renewed vigour within, of uncontrollable feelings of love for all created life, of energized enthusiasm, confidence and zest for living, of a markedly magnified capacity for coping with everyday life and of an appetite for greater truths of the spirit. Regardie himself underwent this process and again summed it up with: 'Thank God!'

The tree of the life he had led at last blossomed to bring forth fruits which nourished his deepest appetites. One ambition was fulfilled during the period under discussion. He had always wanted to write something really helpful for ordinary men and women which would not intimidate them with foreign technical terms nor insist that they believe a dozen improbable things before they are allowed to undertake the first step, which is to lie down on your back on a hard floor. *Be Yourself – The Art of Relaxation* is the ideal present for anyone who suffers from nervous tension. Anyone who can read can understand it. It tells you that life is a wonderful thing and everywhere we see evidence of the inexhaustible energy of nature. So how come you're often tired, irritable, anxious, fatigued or exhausted? You must be doing something wrong. In fact, without knowing it, you are wasting your energy by tensing muscles all over your body. Here are some simple techniques to relieve all the tension. They're fun to do as well. The results are interesting. You will feel more fulfilled. You will have access to an inexhaustible supply of energy if only you be yourself. In order to be yourself, it is first essential to relax.

The exercises can be recommended without the slightest hesitation. Seriously undertaken, they do what they profess to do: they relax one, perhaps more deeply than one has felt in years. All that is required is a hard floor and a vague ability to visualize or at least think about parts of one's own body; although strong visual ability really does speed up the process. The style of the book is spare and clear in every phrase. The author uses the clever stratagem of adopting the tone of *Dr* Regardie and quotes conversations with unnamed patients, in my view a legitimate and in this case truthful literary device for granting to one's matter the stamp of high authority. It works. The reader usually ends the book eager to try Dr Regardie's exciting methods. *Be Yourself – The Art of Relaxation*, is probably the best self-help manual on the matter. It is astonishing that some major paperback publishing corporation did not buy up the rights cheaply a number of years ago and mass market the work in every supermarket and drug-store. It is notable too for the author's sagacious exhortation to adopt the maxim: 'Sit loose to life.'

Regardie expressed his own view of Wilhelm Reich in *Reich: His Theory and Therapy*, a work I have read in manuscript and which, I am delighted to learn, is scheduled for publication. This is by far the finest study of Reich's theory and therapy among the many that jostle for attention and shelf space and it is by a man who underwent it, practised it and drew from extensive clinical experience in his lucid and convincing advocacy of the system's efficaciousness.

At last Regardie felt able to realize an earlier dream: that of uniting Magic with Therapy. He posited the existence of a force which animates all life. This force – or 'God' or 'orgone energy' – can heal and harmonize all which we are. It can transmute us into the divine from the merely 'human, all too human'. However, scientific knowledge is required to activate this force. Like the Alchemist, the Reichian psychotherapist works physically. His hands go to work on your body. Once this force is aroused, the psyche of the person involved demands more of it. This is how magical techniques enter into the matter.

In *Energy, Prayer and Relaxation* which, it will be remembered, was on the second occasion published separately from the original examination of Christian Science and New Thought, Regardie gives his techniques of relaxation, instructs the reader in a more advanced mode of activating energy, and urges that for prayer to be effective, it must be powered by energized enthusiasm within. The essence of the matter is the Middle Pillar Technique. This unites all Regardie's concerns. For its origins, we must return to the Golden Dawn and a document which was circulated among the initiates of its descendant, the Stella Matutina.

> In the aura which interpenetrates and surrounds our physical bodies, we are to build up a replica of the Tree of Life. The Pillar of Severity is on our right side, the Pillar of Mercy is on our left, and the Pillar of Equilibrium in our midst.

It is best to build up the Middle Pillar first. To do this stand up and raise yourself in imagination to your kether – a brilliant light above your head. Imagine this light descending to Daath, at the nape of your neck, and thence to Tiphareth in the heart where it glows like sunlight and whence it radiates into the other sephiroth.

From Tiphareth the light goes to Yesod in the region of the hips, and thence to Malkuth in which your feet are planted.

The student is then instructed to vibrate Hebrew Names of God corresponding to each Sephirah. As Francis King aptly remarks:

It will be obvious to readers that this simple – perhaps deceptively simple – exercise bears at least some resemblance to the tantric process of raising the Kundalini. There is the same emphasis on vivifying psychic centres (and it does not matter whether those centres are called 'chakras' or 'Sephiroth' on the replica of the Tree of Life built up in the aura) and the essence of the two processes is the setting up of a flow of energy through the centre of the 'subtle body'.

There is, however, one very important difference between the two processes. In one, the tantric technique of Layayoga, the energy flow is upward towards the psychic centre which is visualised as being above the crown of the head. In the other, the Middle Pillar Exercise, the flow is exactly reversed, the visualised energy current flowing downwards from the subjective Kether, also conceived of as being above the head (*Tantra for Westerners: A Practical Guide*).

It was Regardie who perceived the many possibilities inherent within this exercise and who did more work on it than anyone else. The Middle Pillar is the spine of *The Middle Pillar* and *The Art of True Healing*. *The Middle Pillar* presents a psychological approach to mind and metaphysics then evolves into a sensible and justified advocacy of certain magical practices, giving clear instruction in the Kabbalistic Cross, the Lesser Banishing Ritual of the Pentagram and obviously the Middle Pillar in addition to the Assumption of God-forms and the Vibration of Divine Names: it is a first-class introduction to basic magical work which is the foundation of all attainment.

The Art of True Healing doesn't waste a word in its crisp exposition of the Middle Pillar technique, as expanded by Regardie. Here is how to do it.

1 Lie down on your back on a hard floor and relax.
2 Breathe slowly, deeply, easily and rhythmically. A cycle of counting 'four' as the breath flows out, as the breath flows in, as the breath is retained and as the breath is expelled is recommended.
3 Now visualize a sphere, roughly four inches in diameter, whirling and glowing with brilliant white light at the crown of the head. Vibrate the Name EHEIEH. Do this for ten cycles of breathing.
4 Visualize light descending to form another sphere at the throat, glowing with ultra-violet light. Vibrate the Name JEHOVOH ELOHIM for ten cycles.
5 Visualize light descending to form another sphere at the solar plexus, its colour being clear pink rose. Vibrate the Name JEHOVOH ELOAH VE-DAATH for ten cycles.
6 Visualize light descending to form another sphere at the genitals, deep purple in colour. Vibrate the Name SHAD-DAI EL CHAI. Again, ten cycles.
7 Visualize light descending to the feet where they form another sphere of rich russet brown. Vibrate the Name ADONAI HA-ARETZ. Ten cycles.
8 Contemplate the Middle Pillar you have established within yourself. Picture the five central Sephiroth as throbbing with energy on this Middle Pillar of brilliant light which connects them. You will now try to circulate the energies aroused.
9 As you breathe out – still maintaining your rhythm – imagine the energy going down the left side of the body from the head to the feet. As you breathe in, it travels up the right side from the feet to the head. Do this not less than four times. Ten is recommended.
10 As you breathe out, imagine the energy pouring down the front of your body from the head to the feet. As you breathe

in, imagine it rippling up the back of your body, from the feet to the head. Do this four or more times.

11 Now throw your attention down to your feet. Imagine the energy rising up through the Middle Pillar to the crown of the head as you breathe in. Then as you breathe out, picture it cascading back down to the feet. Some call this The Fountain Exercise. Do it four or more times.

12 The Exercise of the Interwoven Light: as you breathe in, imagine that a band or bands of brilliant white light are weaving around your body, starting from the feet. Like an Egyptian pharoah, you are being mummified. Continue until your head is finally within the weaving.

13 Express a silent prayer or prayers, using words which mean something to you.

14 You are now able to enjoy fully the glorious sensation of this technique. You may choose simply to bask in the healing and refreshing energies aroused. You may choose to change the colour of the aura around you in order to attract things you might want: there is full instruction on this practice in *The Art of True Healing*.

Regardie insisted that the Middle Pillar is a magnificent multi-purpose tool which anyone with a will can activate relatively easily. Its first benefit is the deep relaxation it induces. One breathes more easily. One feels much more oneself. One brings one's latent powers to life. One directly experiences a phenomenon which can be variously termed 'the life force' or 'God' or 'orgone energy' and which grants one a deepening ecstasy of being which harmonizes the self. Regardie used it to enlighten and guide him: 'I never go to sleep without first lighting the lamp of Kether above my head,' he declared decades after his book first appeared.

An ability to heal others was a third astonishing benefit. He found that if he performed the Middle Pillar prior to seeing a patient, he had access to a force which he could pass on through his hands to their bodies.

In the fourth place, he came to look upon the power aroused

by the technique as the necessary and essential condition of productive magical work. Unless this force was aroused, he argued, the result would be empty posturing. Crowley had termed this power 'energized enthusiasm' and it was Regardie who gave the simplest instructions for its attainment.

One can understand that it is hard for the lay reader to appreciate the excellence of the Middle Pillar process. One can only challenge the open-minded to try it for six months and record the results. If nothing else is accomplished, at least there will be valuable training of the mind in necessary disciplines of memory, visualisation, and concentration: but the present writer would be astonished if six months of daily work did not accomplish some form of rewarding transmutation of the self.

The matter of Talismans will be considered in its proper place: here let it suffice to say that Regardie thought that these objects made in order to realize a desire, can be 'charged' or 'activated' or 'made to work' through a passing of energy aroused by a successful Middle Pillar exercise through the hands and into the talisman, with accompanying one-pointed concentration and rhythmic breathing.

The technique so essential so Regardie argued for effective Magic, was in his opinion indispensable for officers of initiation working under the Golden Dawn system. Unless the inner power was pulsating within the initiatory officers, the ceremony would be worthless: but if the power was present, the officer could pass it on to the candidate, thus activating the part of the psyche which the ritual is designed to bring forth.

There is a further possible application of the Middle Pillar and it is Tantric. However, in the best book on the matter for many years, *Tantra for Westerners: A Practical Guide to the Way of Action*, Francis King discerns a problem in Regardie's rescension of the matter.

Many initiates of the Stella Matutina seem to have been well aware of the 'correspondence-in-reverse' between the Exercise of the Middle Pillar and the tantric process of Kundalini arousal. Thus the late Dr Francis Israel Regardie, at one time Aleister Crowley's secretary but subsequently an initiate of the Stella Matutina, argued that the two processes are only distinguished from one another by one thing, this being that the Middle Pillar Exercise reflects a Western concern with the world of matter and its practicalities, with 'bringing the Divine down into humanity' and spiritualizing the physical, while Kundalini yoga is 'otherworldly', rejects material things and is concerned with divorcing the soul from the flesh and uniting it with the Absolute.

With the greatest respect for Dr Regardie and the many excellent books he wrote - books for which all students of the Golden Dawn owe an enormous debt of gratitude to their author - I think he was mistaken on this matter.

It seems to me that he disregarded the fact that in the Middle Pillar Exercise, however successfully it may be performed and of whatever desirable results it may be productive, *there is no explosive marriage of polarities*. It is true that the energy of the Sahasrara/Kether chakra is transmitted 'downwards' with the object of giving life and power to the other chakras, but there is no transference of *essence*, the inmost being, of the subjective Kether (Shiva, in tantric terminology) to the 'site' of the subjective Yesod, the Muladhara chakra where dwells the serpent power. Nor, of course, is there an 'upward' transference from Yesod to Kether, from the Muladhara to the Sahasrara. And without such a transference of one sort or the other the marriage of opposites cannot be consummated.

With the greatest respect to Francis King and his many excellent books, I think he may well be mistaken on this matter. In my view, there are a number of Tantric elements in the Middle Pillar Exercise as it stands. Firstly, in what I have termed The Fountain Exercise whereby energy is sucked up the Middle Pillar from Malkuth to Kether, thence to cascade in a fountain of showering sparks of light and life, forming an aura as it returns to Malkuth, one is surely employing the polarities of Kether and Malkuth: no wonder that the Kabbalists state that 'Kether is in Malkuth and Malkuth is in Kether but after another manner.' Mr King might object that the use of Malkuth at the feet is inappropriate for Tantric working and I think he would be right: but the problem can be solved by doing The Fountain Exercise, using instead of Malkuth the genital centre of Yesod – also known as the Muladhara chakra.

Secondly, in what has been termed the Exercise of the Interwoven Light, the student is instructed to imagine a band or bands of light arising from Malkuth to mummify the body up to the crown of the head. One way of doing this effectively is to visualize the band of light as being the Serpent of Wisdom of the Kabbala. It is important to pause for a while at Yesod/Muladhara, the genital centre, and identify the Kabbalistic Serpent with the Serpent Power, the Kundalini, of Tantric Yoga, lusting after union with all that exists in Sahasrara/Kether at the crown of the head. Mr King may conceivably have missed these minor points but he has certainly grasped the major issue:

> Nevertheless ... the adaptation of the occidental exercise of the Middle Pillar to tantric purposes is perfectly feasible: the tantric Way of Action in the context of the techniques associated with the Western Esoteric Tradition (*Tantra for Westerners*).

Furthermore, Mr King has indeed done valuable work in specifically applying the Middle Pillar technique to Tantric purposes. Regardie would have warmly welcomed this development, for as he stated in *What You Should Know about the Golden Dawn*: 'However, I do agree entirely with Mr King that the Golden Dawn techniques are capable of almost indefinite expansion. There is much work to be done.'

The Middle Pillar technique is much safer than Kundalini Yoga. Practice of the latter system requires a qualified teacher. Otherwise the persistent student is only too likely to arouse the Serpent Power which will probably arise, vivify the being, get stuck in a lower chakra, induce mania and catapault the seeker into psychosis. This distressing phenomenon occurs because the student has activated more power than his present state of being can handle. Experiments in Kundalini Yoga undertaken while under the influence of powerful, mind-expanding drugs which intensify the ability to visualize, culminate - with dismaying frequency - in the subject acquiring impressive sexual charisma accompanied by messianic convictions, violent behaviour and a delusional system of thought. It can be argued that something of this sort happened to Charles Manson, self-proclaimed messiah and murderer, and ex-member of a degenerate magical order, the Solar Lodge of Los Angeles.

By contrast the Middle Pillar does not require a teacher or guru. There is no danger involved at all. Because the process starts from the top, at Kether/Sahasrara, the centres of power are acting as transformers to bring down the energy. They won't and don't admit more energy than the being can handle.

In the Middle Pillar we have a method for expanding consciousness on every level of awareness and of employing the power activated for all manner of productive purposes. Here Regardie made a major contribution to both Magic and Therapy in his adroit union of the best in both for the good of all. His work has had an important influence upon succeeding generations of students of Magic: one hopes that the wisdom has percolated through to at least some students of psychotherapy. His own constant use of the technique embodied so many of his concerns: expanded consciousness; practical sorcery; Kabbala; Yoga; Magic; healing; and psychotherapy, not to mention Alchemy and orgone energy.

In the course of builing up his practice during the 1950s, Regardie stayed aloof from the occult movement, partly on account of his bitterness over the Crowley quarrel and partly on account of his profound distaste for contact with cranks. He prospered - eventually earning a regular income of the then most munificent sum of 80,000 dollars a year - he enjoyed life and he endeavoured to grapple healthily with its attendant difficulties: he was married and divorced three times with no children. I know nothing of his first marriage. He was reticent too about his second, although a mistress informed me that this wife was a beautiful socialite and his greatest love. Possibly; from what he told me, this last was not my impression. His pithy summary of his third marriage will be related later. More germane to our present purposes is the question of the work he did for those who paid money to consult him.

He was, we recall, a doctor of psychology and a state-licensed chiropracter. Chiropractic is a system of medicine which relies on manual manipulation of the spine to ease pain – one can readily perceive its affinities with Reichian psychotherapy. But to begin with, the majority who went to Regardie required relief from backache. When he cured that, a number were so pleased that they wondered what else he could do for them. If they persisted, they discovered a lay analyst in the Freudian tradition who was also intimately familiar with the Jungian approach and who was furthermore qualified to apply the methods of Reich to ailments far more problematic than backache. These methods were supplemented where necessary by philosophical insight and magical techniques. In other words, Regardie was also what a leading British novelist, Doris Lessing, has termed 'a soul doctor'. Yet he never advertised his magical background. There was no need to advertise at all. Word spread. People came to him. They may have found his treatment unorthodox but it worked – as Chris Monnastre has recorded in her Introduction to the 5th Edition of *The Golden Dawn*.

I entered into Reichian therapy with Regardie for a period of approximately two years. Apart from Reich's method of therapy, he also incorporated some basic pranayama yoga techniques and chiropractic adjustments. But he also occasionally worked at activating one chakra located below my breastbone and above my solar plexus which on the Tree of Life would correspond to Tiphareth. Within a brief time, I felt the 'streamings' referred to by Reich in his writings and others who have experienced this kind of therapeutic work. But the experience of this particular chakra being activated was beyond description! On one occasion I experienced an actual glowing, pulsating sphere within the center of my body which felt like an electrified tennis ball!

Years later, however, I am convinced that this kind of occurrence was not just the result of Regardie's success as a good Reichian therapist, but also due to many years of his own dedicated work with the Middle Pillar technique which he frequently referred to as the 'sine qua non' of all magical work. In other words, Regardie was able, by a kind of process of induction, to begin to open me up to the entrance of powerful healing creative energy from profoundly deep reservoirs of the unconscious (and in the absence of verbal therapy!). Wilhelm Reich had called this energy 'orgone' and, in his opinion, it is what numberless generations before revered and worshipped as 'God'. A Jungian may call this Soul, Self or 'meaning' depending upon individual interpretation. Or a Freudian may relate to this phenomenon as a release of libido. But the Magician calls this experience and influx of energy L.V.X. and with proper training and dedication, is able to release it him or herself WITHOUT THE AID OF AN OUTSIDE PERSON OR AGENCY!

Regardie had a phenemenal ability in generating this kind of energy quickly and efficiently. However, once in 1982 he confided to me that if any person worked the Middle Pillar technique twice daily for a significant period of time, that the same result would eventually occur. If this daily work were combined with sustained relaxation and prolonged rhythmic deep breathing, one could, in effect, *become one's* OWN *'Hierophant'* and trust that one's personal Genius would guide one within the pure intention of sincere effort.

Chris Monnastre first met Regardie in October 1971 and shortly afterwards, as she has related, entered into Reichian therapy with him. By her own account: 'I was too shy to venture any serious questions about the nature of magic, and the few I hinted toward he avoided completely.' The therapy ended in 1974 and for the next five years, although Monnastre and Regardie were in contact, 'he still continued to be reticent regarding any discussion of magical matters'. It wasn't until 1979 that Regardie was prepared to advise the use of the Banishing Ritual of the Pentagram – a clear indication of his mature view that psychotherapy should precede Magic.

There were good reasons for Regardie to keep quiet about his involvement in Magic. He had been appalled by the harassment, suppression and imprisonment of Reich and did not want to share that fate. Nor did he wish to be regarded as a crank. He was sick and tired of receiving letters from self-professed magicians whose words and whose lives supplied evidence of little other than the likelihood of Magic exacerbating already sufficiently severe problems of inflated ego, character armour and emotional plague.

In his inner life, Regardie was doing his True Will – as Crowley would have put it. He was healing human beings and when possible, educating them into knowing the true source of that healing power. In terms of method, he was a logical pragmatist. He used whatever worked, judging the issue through close observation of clinical data. If the technique worked, that was that. If it didn't work, no amount of elegant theorizing could save it from his scornful dismissal.

The conviction took root in him that the Magician must undergo some form of psychotherapy, if the dangerous side-effects of initiation were to be avoided. Contact with other occultists and their glaring display of humourless self-importance and other neuroses continued to appal him. For some decades he held to a self-imposed rule that he would not discuss Magic with a student unless the latter had experience of some method – he didn't care which although he preferred Reichian – of psychotherapy.

It was as though his stripping away of everything other than the essentials of Crowley, Reich, Golden Dawn, Alchemy, psychoanalysis, analytical psychology and the Science and Art of True Healing and the subsequent fruitful, practical combination of these essentials had brought about his own transmutation – *Solve et Coagula* as it is said. He had finally achieved individuation and harmoniously had put it all together.

Which is when there occurred the return of The Beast.

Notes

1 Francis King, 'Wilhelm Reich', in *The Encyclopedia of the Unexplained.*
2 Ibid.

11

'It's a funny old world . . .'

Aleister Crowley and Israel Regardie quarrelled violently shortly after the latter's return to America, it will be recalled. Crowley's horrendous libel caused Regardie to divorce himself from other occultists and to banish the shadow of the man from his consciousness. Given the vicious words which Crowley had written in response to Regardie's own vituperation, one can easily comprehend the lasting anger of the latter. What brought about a change of heart?

Aleister Crowley died in relative poverty and obscurity in Hastings, 1947. Needless to say, Regardie was not among the mourners. Yet in 1951 he bought a biography, *The Great Beast* by John Symonds. Given Regardie's animosity to Crowley, one would have expected him to have been delighted by this hostile and spiteful portrayal. Instead Regardie was galvanized into a reconsideration of everything to do with Crowley, including and especially his own experiences. Despite his many reservations, he was genuinely outraged by Symonds' book:

> It would not be decent to let this opportunity slip by, and let the world continue in its belief that Symonds' horrible account is veridical (*The Eye in the Triangle*).

Fortunately, Regardie was no longer in awe of his former mentor. Through his dedication to the Great Work he had finally acquired that true self-confidence which enables one to reflect on painful experiences and evaluate them objectively. He recognized that the time had come to digest fully all that Crowley had meant to him. His sense of justice was deeply offended by the ignorance and prejudice of Symonds' book which, in its snide and sneering incomprehension, negated all values for which Regardie had struggled so manfully. He felt compelled to write a work intended to restore objectivity, which would give Crowley's ideas balanced consideration and which would also clarify for himself his own ultimate reactions to The Beast.

It took very many years to write this book, which did not appear until 1970 as *The Eye in the Triangle: An Interpretation of Aleister Crowley*. Here he returned to the Magic of his youth but brought to it the wisdom and maturity of age. *The Eye in the Triangle* delights most readers and is considered by most authorities to be by far the finest and most profound study of an extraordinary and controversial figure. Its many insights are of permanent value. It is also a rather strange book and unlike any one has read.

It commences with a personal memoir of Crowley written from the author's contact with him 1928–32. Then it expounds the subject's life and concerns only up until 1914, even though he lived on for another thirty-three years. Why?

> It is my considered belief that he might just as well have died around 1914 and prepared for his next incarnation. Sometimes we all live just a bit too long for our own good. To die early might be the better part of both valor and wisdom.
>
> It is certain that almost all of Crowley's finest creative work was executed before the year 1914. From then on ... he marked time ... his day was done. Thirty more years had to elapse before he was able to shuffle off this mortal coil, but in that period of time he did himself and his reputation incalculable harm. His reputation was not brightened one iota by his life after that date. It is largely for this reason, that I have not taken my story of his pilgrimage beyond the bright period of his highest creativity (*The Eye in the Triangle*).

It does not appear to have struck the author that if Crowley had died in 1914, as he strongly recommended, he could not have met the man to whom, as he confessed, he owed 'everything I am today'. In fact a footnote to the above passage indicates certain doubts as to the wisdom of his own opinion.

I have reflected long on this early observation of mine, and have concluded that it should be modified ... It is possible that circumstances and my conscience may oblige me to write, later, another volume to this work dilating on his later experiences and literary as well as magical career.

It is very unfortunate that this did not occur. Even so, *The Eye in the Triangle* remains a remarkable work. It insists that Crowley was 'A God-intoxicated man', a genuine Magician and Mystic, a beautiful and truthful writer on these matters, an outstanding poet and a great man gifted with genius despite his many personal flaws. He remained an enigma for Regardie. The latter quotes Charles Richard Cammell's *Aleister Crowley: The Man: The Mage: The Poet*: 'Explain to me the riddle of this man!' He keeps trying to strike a balance: praise is often followed by damnation of 'the nasty, petty, vicious louse that occasionally he was on the level of practical human relations'.

Regardie reveals his own concerns as he explains those of Crowley. Much time and space are spent upon the Golden Dawn and the author convincingly demonstrates the central importance of the Order's teachings in the thought and practice of his subject. He observes and applauds Crowley's early struggles to master mind control and Yoga. His understanding of Crowley's experiences in China and after is magnificent. Yet gradually there emerges the desire of Regardie to put Crowley on the couch and give him psycho analysis. This becomes especially evident in the chapter called 'North Africa' in which Regardie analyses and comments on the events which took place in the Sahara, 1909, when Crowley, accompanied by Victor Neuburg, invoked the Aethyrs of Enochian angel-magic, recorded in the document published as *The Vision and the Voice*. The commentator concurs with Crowley's view that these are indeed wondrous and sublime visions; he does not doubt the validity of the experiences, the majesty of the language and the wisdom contained therein, but he nevertheless perceives an area where Crowley failed. To this end he examines the Vision of the 10th

Aethyr which describes an encounter with 'that mighty Devil' Choronzon.

According to Crowley, Choronzon - whose Number is 333 and whose Name means Dispersion - is the Great Demon of the Abyss through which the Adept must pass if one is to be reborn as a Master. According to Regardie, Choronzon is the deepest repressed portion of one's own psyche. He equates it with the symbol of the Devil and in Crowley's case, his unacknowledged father-hatred and Oedipus complex - and the latter's writings are cited in evidence. Regardie argues skilfully that Crowley failed to accept that these destructive energies were within his own psyche; that as a result he was unable to annihilate his ego entirely; and that his crossing of the Abyss was therefore flawed. Perhaps he did indeed manage the crossing - but his ego and his repressed complexes played possum, only to become severely swollen in the years to come. Such is the Regardie thesis here.

It is perfectly possible that Regardie was right. As Crowley wrote in his *Diaries* during the 1940s: 'What an ass I've been!' We have noticed Regardie's preoccupation with the issue of illumination and neurosis. In *The Eye in the Triangle* he endeavoured to resolve the problem:

> That Crowley was illuminated there can be no doubt whatsoever. The more significant doubt that has been brewing in my mind for over three decades is whether his spiritual experience could have resolved his large psychoneurotic problem. It is now my strongest contention that it could not. Crowley's autobiography, as well as the other critical biographies, infer unequivocally that it could not.
>
> A few years ago, I had a pleasant dinner with Mrs Ruth Fuller Sasaki and Dr Henry Platov, both of whom are prominent in the Zen movement in this country, the latter being an authorised Roshi or teacher in this area. After a while the conversation turned to Zen and psychotherapy. Specifically I asked Mrs Sasaki if the Zen disciplinary process (which is not merely a series of philosophical precepts) could cure a psychoneurosis. Emphatically she replied that Zen is not a psychotherapy. The inference is therefore that a frankly neurotic

personality can co-exist with the highest illumination, the attainment of the Prajna Paramita.

On later occasions, discussing this problem with Dr Platov, he took a somewhat different view that the different *satoris*, or illuminations, over a period of time may gradually heal the neurotic 'lesion', if we may so call it, and tend to integrate the personality. In a Zen monastery, if a candidate presented a frank neurosis which markedly interfered with his acquiring the needed meditative skills, he would either be dismissed or asked to consult another Roshi, perhaps housed in the same monastery, for a species of psychotherapy; showing a clear realization that *Satori* however profound does nothing to the neurosis itself.

According to Regardie, Crowley was indeed a Master but one disfigured, so to speak, by the most unsightly blemishes, blisters, scars, pimples and boils. Crowley's probable answer to this charge is contained in his *The Book of Lies*, Chapter 40, THE HIMOG - HIMOG being a Notariqon of the words Holy Illuminated Man of God.

THE HIMOG

A red rose absorbs all colours but red; red is therefore the one colour that it is not.
This Law, Reason, Time, Space, all Limitation blinds us to truth.
All that we know of Man, Nature, God, is just that which they are not: it is that which they throw off as repugnant.
The HIMOG is only visible in so far as He is imperfect.
Then are they all glorious who seem not to be glorious, as the HIMOG is All-glorious Within?
It may be so.
How then distinguish the inglorious and perfect HIMOG from the inglorious man of earth?
Distinguish not!
But thyself Ex-tinguish: HIMOG art thou, and HIMOG shalt thou be.

In his penultimate chaper, 'Attitudes', Regardie is still

grappling with the problem of understanding the nature of The Beast. The tone throughout is one of ambivalence. At times the author appears determined to put Crowley down: several sentences later, there is an enraptured paean of praise. He keeps assuring the reader that his subject had many faults which he did not miss and he does this every time he overdoes the appreciation. He also keeps assuring the reader that Crowley was a genius of the spirit and he does this every time he overdoes the criticism.

This ambivalence was also reflected in Regardie's behaviour in 1981–2. He sometimes liked to startle timid, 'spiritual' guests – the word 'spiritual' surely suggests some nauseating commercial brand of camomile tea – by striding around his home proclaiming: 'Do what thou wilt shall be the whole of the bloody law,' and I'd cheerfully chime in with: 'Love is the law, love under bleeding will.' Feeble 'New Age' people would be treated to a long, rational lecture on the virtues of Crowley. Yet over-earnest and excessively devout Crowleyans found him even more shocking. Pious disciples were only too likely to be told at dinner: 'You see, the one thing about Crowley which took me years to understand was his occasional desire for women to piss and shit on him. Can't say I ever shared his taste myself – but the old man used to love it!'

By this time, Regardie had established a formidable reputation in his own right: as I remarked to his secretary; '*he's* the old man now.' Yet he freely and openly admitted, without the slightest embarrassment, that Crowley's attainments were far greater than his own. He recognized that he owed him a debt. As we noted in the first chapter of this work, Regardie always endeavoured to behave honourably. He proceeded to edit a succession of Crowley's works for publication: *Book Four*, which still impressed him; *Three Holy Books* whose beauty had moved him; *AHA!* a mystical poem which still thrilled him; *The Vision and the Voice*, which made him wonder; *The World's Tragedy*, which demonstrates his complete repudiation of Christianity in the editor's expressed concurrence with the author; *The Best of Crowley*, which consists of the literary pieces he loved most; *Magick Without Tears*, which he had initially found lamentable and came to find laudable; and above all else, *Gems from the Equinox: All the Magical Writings*.

He really did feel a need to place Crowley's theory, practice and general wisdom before the public. An Introduction accompanied each edition. There seems to be among students of Crowley and his many commentators an unspoken competition in the art of writing Introductions to his work. Perhaps surprisingly, the competition is stiff. Connoisseurs of this matter applaud Francis King, commend Stephen Skinner, appreciate the pithy words of Gerald Yorke, deplore the nonsense of the Metaphysical Research Group, sigh wearily over Kenneth Grant and John Symonds and cheer for Regardie. His essays are consistently stimulating. He explains the nature of the book, informs the reader about the author's life and ideas, insists upon the value of the work, brings in his own personal perspective, recommends further reading and comments sagaciously.

Reconsideration of Crowley inevitably involved reconsideration of *The Book of the Law. The Eye in the Triangle* has a chapter on the matter. Regardie's difficulty lay in accepting that it was dictated by an independent, praeter-human intelligence. He accepted, in common with even the most hostile who have studied the matter, that *The Book of the Law* is not the *conscious* composition of Aleister Crowley. Given the nature of Regardie's studies in Psychology, the hypothesis he advances is both possible and predictable. He argues – and argues well – that Aiwass, who dictated the document, is ultimately the Highest Self of the many selves which made up Crowley, identical with what the Golden Dawn called 'the Higher Genius'. Not that this invalidates *The Book of the Law*. In Regardie's view, the Higher Genius within Crowley, expressing itself through the man's imaginative, intellectual and personal involvements, his emotional preoccupations, his sexual drives and his spiritual concerns, wrote a document of unique importance for humankind.

Regardie had finally come to realize the essential identity

between the views of Reich and 'Do what thou wilt shall be the whole of the law.'

'Do what thou wilt' has no meaning other than this ... The physical organism functions on this basis. Homeostasis is the law which regulates its activities ... It has its own inherent laws by means of which it functions. Psychologically, the same is true. Man has always had thrust on him moral codes which seek to tell him how he should behave under this and that or the other circumstance, instead of helping the living person to function spontaneously. By so doing, one falls back instinctively on a non-verbal and non-rational code which has enabled the organism-as-a-whole to survive over millions of years and evolve into its present state. No arbitrary moral code was responsible for this. Survival is the integral property of the living person.

Reich was another advocate of the notion of the self-regulatory function of the human being. He claimed that if the infant were not basically interfered with biologically by having neurotic parental standards forcibly imposed upon it, it would be able to be wholly self-determining throughout its entire lifetime. When first introduced to this idea, most people stand aghast at it – as if any individual would 'go completely to hell' if permitted to express itself freely on an animal or biological level. I have heard parents say that if they let junior select his own foods, for example, they would consist solely of chocolate bars and pop. At first, this sounds *almost* as if it could be so – until one becomes familiar with some basic experimental work (*The Eye in the Triangle*).

Regardie proceeds to quote an interesting set of laboratory experiments. A group of children whose ages ranged from six months to three years was confronted every feeding time by trays containing small portions of up to thirty different foodstuffs. The children who could talk said what they wanted; those who couldn't speak pointed. If food was rejected, even if it was spat out, no attempt was made to force or cajole the child into eating.

Selection, apparently, was made on the basis of visual and olfactory interests. At the close of the experiments, after some months, it was determined that the selection of foods, so far as concerned basic food elements such as minerals, vitamins, proteins, etc. would not be other than would have been prescribed by a nutritional expert. In other words, the infant selected - it was not cajoled. There was no imposition of authoritarian dictates - no matter how sound or reliable. The infant was permitted to select on a spontaneous natural basis - and it prospered.

It is obvious here that Regardie has resolved another dilemma: his ultimate attitude to Freud. In common with Reich, he agreed with Freud that 'God' is a name for the sex instinct, which is the libido and which drives us: in common with Crowley, he came to agree that the sex instinct is God. Therefore he disagreed with Freud's notion that repression is necessary if there is to be civilization. So did Reich, who thought that repression is responsible for all the ills of society. So did Crowley, who declared with *The Book of the Law* that 'The word of Sin is Restriction'. In *The Eye in the Triangle*, Regardie enthusiastically endorsed Crowley's libertarian sexual attitudes which he supported by citing Reich.

Although his attitude to Crowley grew more positive with each passing year, it remained tempered by open questioning and cold criticism. Some portion of his mind returned repeatedly to attacking the problem of a just evaluation of the man. I recall asking Regardie: 'Was Crowley kind?' He looked quite startled. Then he frowned and pondered the question as though he'd never thought about it before. Minutes passed. Finally he stated quietly: 'Yes ... yes ... yes, he was kind.' These words were uttered in a tone of puzzled surprise.

His return match with a now disembodied Crowley affected him deeply. It was the last thing he had expected. He had been leading a joyful and fulfilling life. His income satisfied all comforts and purchased such luxuries as he desired. He had no plans to continue as a writer – once he had written on Crowley, he considered that he had finally said all that he had to say publicly. He could see daily evidence of the success of his art in the happy faces of the patients he was healing. He was enjoying an active and healthy sex life: and the company of stimulating, warm and intelligent friends from all walks of life. He had no intention of embarking on a disciplined programme of extra work. His income and his reputation were secure. After all, when *The Eye in the Triangle* first appeared in 1970, Regardie was sixty-three, an age when most people, to use his words, are 'fairly well played out … The Fires of life are beginning to dim if not go out altogether.'

Instead there followed seventeen years of arduous but productive labour. He perceived that Crowley's acid critique of psychoanalysis was accurate: that it was a misguided restoration, in twentieth-century parlance, of the Christian doctrine of Original Sin, a concept which Crowley and Reich and Regardie disgustedly repudiated. Perhaps more importantly, he sorted out within himself his relationship to Crowley purely as a writer on Magic. He had long since banished from his style any mannered endeavour to sound 'learned' or 'educated' – which had led in his early endeavours to unnecessarily complex phrasing – and agreed with Orwell that clarity is the key. He had his own wisdom and did not need to stand on Crowley's shoulders. He discerned and accepted his own skills and his own limitations. Crowley was always complaining that his readers failed to understand him and much of the time he had only himself to blame: Regardie did not suffer from any such difficulty. Although Crowley's obscurities tend to be worth the effort of close scrutiny, they are irritatingly deliberate, as though he were self-consciously writing for an elite: Regardie took pains to make his matter clear even to the dullest reader. Students of Magic find that Crowley gives the most succinct instructions: but one has to turn to Regardie if one wants to know *why* they are as they are. Finally, Regardie has his own unique perspective on magical matters and his introduction of psychology is in the present writer's view a contribution of lasting importance. In the course of concluding *The Eye in the Triangle* Regardie wrote:

Crowley was not merely a man of the world, nor yet a distinguished literary man nor a mystic of considerable attainment. Against his will, he had been transformed into a Man with a Message for the whole of mankind.

One cannot resist wondering whether something similar was happening to Regardie. On the last page of *The Eye in the Triangle*, with seventeen years of life to come, Regardie summarizes his view of *The Book of the Law*.

It really makes little difference in the long run whether the Book was dictated by a praeterhuman intelligence named Aiwass or whether it stemmed from the creative deeps of Aleister Crowley. The Book was written. And he became the mouthpiece for the *Zeitgeist*, accurately expressing the intrinsic nature of our time as no one else has done to date. So his failures and excesses and stupidities are simply the hallmark of his humanity. Was he not, by his own admission, the Beast, whose number is 666, which is the number of Man?

He closes the work by quoting with approval Crowley's impassioned advocacy of *The Book of the Law*. In time he would edit and write a splendid Introduction to it, published as *The Law Is For All*. The very idea of doing this would have evoked his acerbic disbelief if expressed in, say, 1947. As he viewed the Sixties, Seventies and Eighties and the changes in his own being which they brought about, time and time again he shook his head ruefully, smiled wryly and exclaimed: 'It's a funny old world ...'

12

The Occult Explosion

Something strange happened during the 1960s which is still the subject of examination, analysis and debate. It is not my purpose here to grapple with a deep, difficult and profoundly interesting subject but it is necessary to indicate its essentials. There was in the West a mass movement towards an expansion of consciousness and in quest of evolutionary growth. This manifested in many ways, some of which were simply silly. The era was a paradise for posers. It was also a joy to be alive then.

Most Westerners were better off materially than in the memory of mankind. There was unprecedented leisure time. Any able-bodied, common-sensical adult could obtain paid employment which would give him acceptable food and shelter with enough money left for a few luxuries. There had never been so many institutions of further education and higher learning bringing so many young, intelligent and creative people together.

Many expressed their dissatisfaction with materialism and looked for something more deeply satisfying to the spirit. The beatniks – originally of San Francisco but later of New York, London, Paris, Rome and other American and European cities – had already professed themselves to be alienated from the tawdry concerns of the herd and of the sordid struggles for empty status in the society around them. Their successors, the hippies, shared this view but advanced it in rather less intellectual terms. Whereas the beatniks had communed mainly with the sweet fumes of marijuana, the hippies added to this heady intake hallucinogens such as the psyllocybillin mushroom, mescaline – the active ingredient of the peyote cactus – and above all, the chemically manufactured substance LSD-25. Ingestion of these drugs caused profound and largely pleasurable changes in consciousness. Use of drugs spread to the more adventurous members of the respectable middle classes and became popular with the decadent upper class and disreputable working class. The upshot of the matter is that people took powerful mind-altering drugs, these threw them into what were usually blissful or at worst instructive states and these experiences prompted them to seek for ways of understanding what had transpired. Many turned to Eastern Religions. Yoga and Zen enjoyed a boom, after which Sufism was marketed. Some turned to Magic and the occult. There was a demand for ways which could induce the ecstatic drug experience without drugs.

All this was accompanied by something which has been termed 'The Permissive Society' or 'The Sexual Revolution'. The latter phrase has been misunderstood. The sexual mores of Westerners changed little. They had sex as much as ever – only they stopped feeling guilty about the fact. There was also a return to the traditional custom – which upstart middle-class and muddled Victorian thinking had for a century interrupted – of teenage sexual relations. This attitude gave the period a climate of exciting freedom and an ever-present sense of expanding boundaries.

In England it seemed as though every maladroit aspect of its hallowed class system was being gleefully tossed into the refuse heap. In America there were unprecedented mass protests against the system of education, the Vietnam War and the insidiously totalitarian 'military-industrial complex' alleged to run the country to the immense dissatisfaction of its citizens. In France, the students of Paris brought down Charles De Gaulle and told a hero it was time he went home. In Czechoslovakia there was a joyous repudiation of sullen tyranny and a collective endeavour to build 'socialism with a human face', a movement swiftly suppressed by brutal Soviet military force.

So many individuals sought after ways of transmuting the human consciousness into the divine state of being to which certain drugs had introduced them. This quest unfortunately evoked the publication of far too many worthless books on various aspects of 'spirituality': but at least some were good and would probably not have been reprinted without this undiscriminating demand. Aleister Crowley's books, which were expensive and as hard to locate as the work of a Russian dissident, were at last reprinted in cheaper editions. Regardie experienced the same fate. Both authors gained a growing reputation with a new generation. Whatever their differences, there was one essential factor in common. Both of them really knew what they were writing about.

A new figure appeared on the scene: Dr Timothy Leary. Leary was a Harvard psychologist who had investigated the effects of LSD. In the course of this he observed that the medical uses of the substance included the most effective cure for alcoholism ever recorded; and the best results yet noted in the rejuvenation of institutionalized elderly people classified as 'hopeless' and waiting to die. He noticed too a principal effect upon an ordinary person: ecstasy and an appetite for metaphysics: a consequence, it will be remembered, of successful psychotherapy. This led him to advocate the widespread use of LSD which he at that time perceived as a universal panacea. He coined the slogan: *Turn on. Tune in. Drop out.*

Leary was not actually advocating a *modus operandi* of drug-dominated uselessness. '*Drop out*' does not mean 'Be a lazy bum'. It meant that one should drop out of taking trivial matters seriously – such as artificial games of status and the obsessive and unsatisfying pursuit of new technological toys, many of them marketed for no more useful purpose than a display of their owner's socio-economic position. Leary's quest was for higher consciousness and more rewarding patterns of human behaviour. He identified the key as being human intelligence, a conclusion on which he was in accord with the Renaissance magi and their Hermetic Wisdom, and he sought after ways of increasing it. His techniques combined drugs and mysticism. His *The Psychedelic Experience* is a sober yet stimulating work which advocates the use of *The Tibetan Book of the Dead* for a profitable structuring of an LSD experience and it has not yet received its just measure of appreciation.

Unsurprisingly Dr Leary was yet another victim of the emotional plague. His opinions were consistently misrepresented to the detriment of his intellectual reputation and his personal character was vilified. Eventually he was arrested, charged, found guilty and sentenced to ten years' imprisonment, which would include lengthy periods of solitary confinement, for the heinous crime of being found in possession of a laughably small quantity of marijuana. When he escaped from prison, the CIA devoted its resources to his recapture, finally kidnapping him in Algeria so as to return him to a maximum security gaol for murderers, rapists and gangsters. Eventually, growing and voluble outrage among leading members of the American intelligentsia procured Leary's release.

Smiling as though his ordeal had not occurred, Leary returned to public life but with the realization that LSD alone is not enough. He explored and continues to explore the potential within humankind with benefit to all who pay attention to his data and hypotheses. Curiously enough, he feels a strong affinity with Crowley. According to Kenneth Grant:

> Timothy Leary, for example, identifies himself so entirely with the current initiated by Crowley, and the 'coincidences- synchronicities between my life and his', that he considers one of his aims to be the completion of the work of preparing the world for cosmic consciousness, which Crowley had begun (Preface to *The Confessions*).

Regardie came to know Leary and this contact stimulated his productivity. At times the extent of his involvement worried him. He had no desire to suffer as Crowley, Reich and Leary had suffered: he had surely suffered enough. He dreaded the attention of the authorities. He tried to avoid the public eye, he refused invitations to broadcast on the radio or to appear on television and he endeavoured to minimize what was in fact a revolutionary position. Nevertheless he felt sufficiently moved to pen a strong Introduction to a Crowley compilation from *The Equinox*, published in one volume as *Roll Away the Stone*. This consists of a pharmacological essay on the properties of cannabis by a noted pharmacist, E. P. Whineray, who supplied the herb to Crowley in pre-1914 London; Crowley's essay *The Psychology of Hashish*; Crowley's translation of a Baudelaire essay on the subject; and an interesting description of the effects of the drug by an obscure but skilful American writer. Regardie's Introduction encourages the use of mind-expanding drugs for willed magical and mystical purposes and deplores their undisciplined abuse. The essay makes the necessary point that Crowley's employment of drugs was usually aimed at the accomplishment of a specific goal, and it was not merely fatuous self-indulgence. It contemplates the hippies, welcomes their presence insofar as they can make genuine contact with vital energies and age-old truths, sighs briefly over the fact that the hippies expressed these truths as though they alone had discovered them and sternly rejects the notion of Crowley as a Victorian hippie.

Regardie observes that at least two factors sharply distinguish Crowley from the hippies. Firstly he was not an advocate of promiscuous peace to one and all. He discerned no evidence that we live in an Age of Peace. To him it seemed only too obvious that this is the Age of War, of War's God Horus, as *The Book of the Law* states. Regardie recognized the fact that Crowley would have disdained and dismissed the loudly proclaimed dissolution of all aggressive feelings which the hippies hypocritically announced.

Secondly, as Regardie emphasizes, Crowley would soon have lost patience with the hippies' lack of self-discipline. The all too frequent morass of fine words followed by shabby actions would have led him to share the contempt of the punks. Too many hippies did little more than chain-smoke joints while sitting in a circle listening to boring, self-indulgent music while pontificating between puffs on allegedly profound truths of the body, mind and spirit on which they intended to do some practical work shortly after the middle of the following week provided they could get it together, man. The movement swiftly degenerated as its original impetus was weakened by adulteration. It folded fast in face of tough opposition. Those who preached peace and love at rallies professed to be astounded and disillusioned when their smiles were answered by the authorities with the crunch of a police club thrust through the teeth. Many shocked their nervous systems into psychosis or permanent nervous affliction by taking too much LSD too often. The most bitterly disillusioned destroyed themselves with heroin. Today there is no creature sadder than a mild, bemused, burned-out, ageing hippie.

Regardie endorsed Crowley's views on drugs while deploring the former's addiction to heroin in 1920–6 and 1939–47. His Introduction stresses that drugs are just tools for the exploration and enhancement of consciousness. Their use can be very pleasurable. Each drug should be employed for a specific purpose and used with intelligence and will. Moreover, if the purpose is anything other than purely hedonistic, the dose and the results should be recorded. All drugs should be legal for all adults although they are not and Regardie would not advise anyone to break the law: he suggests offering oneself as a guinea-pig for legal psychological experimentation as being a way around the problem. Abuse of drugs is obviously foolish but the harm done can be remedied if there is sufficient will-power and self-discipline. Finally, an intelligent use of chemical substances directed by the will can assist the evolution of human consciousness when supplemented by Magical and psychotherapeutic practice.

Although Regardie watched the hippies with initial enthusiasm followed by increasingly acid comment, he retained his detachment. Drugs, after all, were nothing new to him. In the 1950's he had experimented with LSD under controlled laboratory conditions – 'Thank God!' he exclaimed once again – and he enjoyed the effects of cannabis. At the age of 76 he would serve coffee, cognac and powerful hash cookies for those diners at his home who wanted them, including himself. He told me that he loved to take LSD once a year in solitude and gaze with gladness upon the surrounding scenery. 'But I've never had much use for cocaine. Only tried it a few times and it did absolutely nothing for me.'

Although mass interest in the occult waned during the 1970s there was nevertheless a minor but growing demand for good books on Magic. Regardie responded, as has been noted, with admirable work for the advancement of Crowley but he had also established himself as an authority in his own right. His earlier works were now reprinted with new Introductions written in the light of experience. He did not expect to be asked for more.

He answered this unexpected demand by putting together the foundations of practical Magic in *Twelve Steps to Spiritual Enlightenment*, later reprinted as *The One Year Manual*. This is an outstanding textbook of sound magical practice. Anyone who does not master the techniques the author prescribes and who then attempts more advanced work is asking for trouble and attracting disaster. One can erect an effective and versatile *modus operandi* on the basis of this book. Regardie also wrote two excellent practical manuals for the 'Paths to Inner Power' series of the English Aquarian Press: *A Practical Guide to Geomantic Divination* and *How to Make and Use Talismans*.

The former is precisely what its title proclaims. Geomancy was Regardie's favourite form of Divination. He had learned it from the Golden Dawn and he persistently employed it with rewarding results. The method is of Earth. According to Regardie, it gives practical answers to practical questions. The diviner voices the question and concentrates upon it, then makes lines of dots, either with a stick which prods the sand or with a pencil which marks the paper. The dots are interpreted in terms of odd and even numbers which enable one to construct a series of hieroglyphs which have meaning and which relate to Astrology, Kabbala and other ways of classifying and evaluating the data of the human psyche. The I-Ching uses 64 symbols; the Tarot functions in terms of 10 minor and 22 major numbers, making 32 which is half of 64; and geomancy halves the number again by making use of 16 symbols. The present writer has experimented with geomancy and although he was never particularly attracted to the method, it was found useful for the perceptive analysis of immediate and practical affairs. He has also witnessed Regardie's application of geomancy to questions of this nature and can attest to the accuracy of the technique when in the hands of a leading proponent of its worth.

How to Make and Use Talismans might strike the casual observer as being a candidate for that section of the bookshelf which one mentally labels 'Cranks' Corner'. In fact, it is a calm, clear and logical manual. It propounds the view that we can get what we need and should get what we need if only we go about it in an appropriate way. The way suggested is that of making an object on which we inscribe words and symbols corresponding to the need in question. These objects are called talismans. Regardie's manual gives straightforward guidance on how to go about the matter, suggests simplifying and sensible innovations of technique based upon experience and records, and advocates two methods of 'charging' the talisman so as to render it effective: the Middle Pillar technique and the ceremonial practice taught in the Golden Dawn. Anyone who wants to know how to make and use talismans cannot afford to be without the book.

In 1980, the Falcon Press (in the USA) and the Aquarian Press (in the UK) published Regardie's *Ceremonial Magic: A Guide to the Mechanisms of Ritual.* This altogether splendid work was the solution to a problem which had long perplexed its author. He had indeed published the Golden Dawn teachings – but how were isolated individuals to put these into practice? It might be possible through repeated use of the Middle Pillar to initiate oneself as a Neophyte under the Golden Dawn system. But how could one take this further in the absence of a chartered initiatory group? Regardie's solution was akin to that of Crowley: the student must self-initiate. On the next step, Crowley and Regardie parted company. Crowley dismissed the Golden Dawn initiations of Zelator (Earth), Theoricus (Air), Practicus (Water) and Philosophus (Fire) as a tiresome, long-winded parade of the recondite occult knowledge of Mathers. Regardie thought this inaccurate and unfair. He perceived magical merit in these rituals and so he turned his attention to devising ways in which the student could gather up their concentrated benefits while working alone.

In *Ceremonial Magic*, Regardie advances for our attention a ritual of self-initiation which can be adapted to the purposes of the Golden Dawn initiations between Neophyte and Adeptus Minor. His Opening by Watchtower, which draws upon years of patient experimentation and intimate knowledge of the advanced Enochian System is set forth simply. All words and gestures receive clear explanation. It is then revealed that this recommended ritual is simply the bare bones of the matter, Flesh and blood pulsate in the *First Elaboration*, burn in the *Second Elaboration* and come to potential orgasmic climax in the *Completed Ritual*. Instruction is then given for the consumption of the Magical Eucharist, which should invigorate the imbiber, and the reader is adeptly advised on *Equipment and Paraphernalia*. All this is surely sufficient – compared to the paucity of useful information and plethora of padding in too many magical textbooks – but in Part Two the author examines, analyses and encourages the use of *The Bornless Ritual*. This rite came from a 'fragment of a Graeco-Egyptian work upon Magic, from a papyrus in the British Museum, edited for the Cambridge Antiquarian Society, with a translation by Charles Wycliffe Goodwin, 1852'. Although its use was never specifically advised in the Golden Dawn, it was circulated among the Adepti. Crowley grew to love it and to employ it frequently in his own work. Through its use he finally obtained the Knowledge and Conversation of his Holy Guardian Angel in 1906. In Cefalu 1921, after many years of experimentation, he wrote his final rescension of the ritual and a detailed 'scholation' for a disciple, Frank Bennett/Frater Progradior. In *Ceremonial Magic*, Regardie brings the matter more down to earth for the aspirant. He points out the way in which anyone with sufficient dedication can, through the Opening by Watchtower done repeatedly and The Bornless

One done repeatedly, achieve the equivalent of the Golden Dawn Adeptus Minor Grade, while working in solitude.

The work contains an additional delight. In the Appendices there is a brilliant essay on *The Bacchae* of Euripides, written in the mid-1930s, and examining and exhorting its use as a powerful magical ritual. Other Appendices give two versions of *The Bornless One* – the original and Crowley's adaptation – and the rituals of the Pentagram and Hexagram. Regardie suggests that the student switches from the traditional Hexagram of two triangles in various juxtapositions to the Unicursal Hexagram, constructed from one continuous line and pioneered by Crowley; this suggestion is based on his own work with both. *Ceremonial Magic* therefore provides the aspirant with all the information required for productive years of ritual practice.

The publication of new books and the reprinting of old ones brought Regardie very little money. It also brought him the sort of attention which he did not welcome. Lunatics pestered him with mad correspondence. His days often began with epistolary insults. Sometimes he was provoked into penning impatient replies and even into making these public. One graceless missive of vulgar abuse was countered with the words: 'I've been told that you're a snot-nosed kid. Get back to your mother's tit – for just a little while longer!' In time he assembled a collection which he called *Liber Nuts*. I read this in manuscript, it has to be seen to be believed, and one doesn't know whether to laugh or to cry over human folly. I am glad to learn, however, that it is scheduled for publication by Falcon Press. Occultists are in serious need of comic relief.

It says much for Regardie's sense of humour that he was able to laugh, albeit ruefully, over two burglaries of his Los Angeles home. Dishonourable idiots invaded to steal rare works of Crowley and notable Golden Dawn items. Strangely enough, he regarded this upsetting experience as being a karmic penalty for anything he might have done wrongly in his youth; at the same time, these events influenced his decision to leave Los Angeles in 1981.

He had discharged his duty to Crowley. He had given all he could give as a practical instructor. He had done his will and his work as a healer. Surely nothing more remained? Surely he was now entitled to a cushy retirement? To his occasional annoyance and continuous perplexity there remained one further and horribly demanding obligation.

The Golden Dawn.

13

Light in Extension

The Golden Dawn was reprinted and kept in print during the 1970s. This time it sold quite briskly, despite its high price. It continued to inspire individuals to take up the Great Work and in some cases to correspond with the editor. He turned in his chiropracter's licence in 1981 at the age of seventy-four and moved to a luxurious home in the beautiful artists' colony of Sedona, Arizona. There, in the words of his friend Dr Christopher Hyatt: 'Until recently he has lived in relative seclusion spending his time writing and relaxing. On occasion he travels and entertains guests at his home.'[1]

He made friendly contact with Dr Robert Anton Wilson, author of *The Cosmic Trigger, Prometheus Rising* and other outstanding works of consciousness expansion. Regardie called him 'a *mindblower*'; and Wilson wrote a notable Introduction to the 3rd edition of *The Eye in the Triangle*, which he praised as 'a masterpiece of exposition'. Other friends included psychologists, magicians, artists, writers, a Zen Master and a gangster. Another notable was US Army Major Grady McMurtry, who had been a disciple of Crowley in the 1940s. Crowley had given McMurtry 'Caliphate' powers for the Ordo Templi Orientis (OTO): that is to say, in the event of the OTO being in danger of withering and dying, McMurtry was entitled to lead a revival as 'Caliph'. When it seemed as though this eventuality had come to pass, McMurtry contacted Regardie and Gerald Yorke – whom he perceived as 'The Eyes of Horus' and guardians of Crowley's legacy – and asked for their approval of his action in activating the powers of the Caliphate: both gave their approval. Major McMurtry then spearheaded an OTO revival from his base in Berkeley, California, conducted the affairs of the Caliphate OTO to the satisfaction of its members and died in 1985, leaving behind him a growing and fruitful organization which has recently been granted recognition as *the* OTO in a US Federal court.

Regardie never joined the OTO, though he wished it well and enjoyed warm and friendly relations with McMurtry, who gave him many presents of rare Crowley books, inscribed with respect and affection. Contrary to opinions one has often heard expressed, McMurtry and the Caliphate OTO did not condemn the Golden Dawn on account of the sentence in *The Book of the Law*: 'Behold! the rituals of the old time are black.' The Caliph argued in *The Magical Link*, the OTO journal, that the words apply to Christianity and Magic based on Christian formulae. As long as the point of view was not anti-Thelemic, McMurtry welcomed work at the Golden Dawn system and viewed any development of it as a functioning Order with benevolence.

Regardie's relationship with Gerald Yorke now moved from their former 'distant-friendly' chats to distant-friendly correspondence. Yorke had also repudiated Crowley as a Master and World Teacher though he had remained his lifelong friend and guardian of his papers: his own quest had led him to embrace Tibetan Buddhism and he had become the Dalai Lama's Representative in the West. This led him to stress the efficaciousness of the Tibetan Buddhist way and deplore that of the Golden Dawn in a lacklustre Introduction to Ellic Howe's *The Magicians of the Golden Dawn*. Regardie wrote to Yorke recording his firm disagreement with the latter's views and warning him that in the review of Howe's book which he was writing, he would attack him: Yorke responded by quoting *The Book of the Law*; 'As brothers fight ye!'

By the end of the 1970s, it appeared as though the only groups working as Golden Dawn Orders were located in New Zealand and in Georgia, USA. However in 1981 Regardie was approached by a woman he had known for some years and who had persuaded him to give her magical instruction. She proposed the establishment of a Golden Dawn Temple in Los Angeles. Initially, Regardie gave her very little encouragement. His experience of group working had left him feeling disillusioned and he preferred to extol the virtues of private individual practice. Finally, he reluctantly acceded to her request to act as consultant in case of difficulty.

The Temple was duly set up by three people whom we shall call Ms B. – its moving spirit – Ms J. and Mr Y., and one cannot doubt their sincerity in endeavouring to work the Golden Dawn system in a formal context. Nor can one doubt their dedication to Magic or their skills. The Temple attracted a variety of individuals from all manner of socio-economic backgrounds and charged a subscription of just five dollars a month. It followed Regardie in insisting that its members undergo some form of psychotherapy. During the period that the present writer was an active member, no grandiose claims were made and the Order was run efficiently and well.

I was present on one occasion when Ms B. came to Regardie for some advice. She alleged that two members had been talking to her about something called Morality and the Magical Path and suggesting that moral guidelines be given to members for the conduct of their private lives. Regardie was horrified. 'No!' he snapped. 'Out of the question! Tell those people they're idiots.' And he quoted MacGregor Mathers: 'What I discountenance and will check and punish wherever I find it in the Order is the attempt to criticise and interfere with the private life of Members of the Order ... The private life of a person is a matter between himself and herself and his or her God ...'

The LA Temple flourished for a time before suffering the fate which strikes so many magical organizations: personality clashes. Ms J. and Mr Y. withdrew, as did a numbers of others, and in time they founded their own Temple. Ms B. continued with her adherents, and forged a link with the Temple in Atlanta, Georgia, in addition to two which sprang into existence in Las Vegas, Nevada and San Diego, California. Both Los Angeles Temples made contact with New Zealand. Nor was England immune from the Golden Dawn revival. Two Temples at least have been going well since 1985; a third has recently been established in London; and there may be others quietly pursuing their work.

The magical revival of the 1980's meant, among other things, that Regardie received letters from all over the world and he always endeavoured to answer them. Some of this correspondence was rewarding; and as we have noticed, some was definitely not. There was also his devotion to his own magical practices. This led to an interior revelation which has been described by Christopher Hyatt:

> While in an exalted state he once experienced an array of religious insists which encompassed him, finally bringing him to a state of exhilaration and collapse where the only thing left in his mind was the following, 'not Christianity, not Buddhism, not Paganism, not anything but the *Golden Dawn*, the System which encompasses all.' I was present when he experienced this revelation and can clearly testify to its intensity and meaning.[2]

It was perhaps on account of this insight that Regardie went to work in his seventies on preparing a new edition of *The Golden Dawn* for publication by Hyatt's Falcon Press. It wasn't a question of any money which might accrue to Regardie: it will be remembered that he had long ago signed away any and all rights to financial gain. To his mind it was a question of honourable obligation. The teachings of the Golden Dawn had become the spine of his interior life. The number of Golden Dawn Temples was growing slowly but steadily; there was evidence of a genuine revival which would be corroborated within a few years. Christopher Hyatt was convinced that 'the number of unaffiliated devotees of the Golden Dawn probably runs into the hundreds of thousands'.[3] Even if the figure is far too optimistic, there was nevertheless a growing demand and therefore a growing sale of good books on Magic. Regardie therefore felt inwardly compelled to devote his old age to making available all Golden Dawn material at his disposal and to which he had access and commenting with all the wisdom he had gained in the light of forty years' experience for the edification of posterity.

He often found the work arduous, tiring and irksome. 'I'm hoping – almost against hope – that some of my drive may return to force me to get back to the job of re-writing the Golden Dawn,' he wrote to me on 21 January 1982. *The Complete Golden Dawn System of Magic* finally appeared in late 1984. It is a massive tome of more than one thousand pages. 'I am glad you got the new Golden Dawn,' Regardie remarked in his letter to me of 13 November 1984, for he had very kindly sent me a copy; 'It is an immense volume, valuable as a good door stop.' In fact, Regardie had every reason to be proud of his achievement. The work is the definitive, harmonious synthesis of Magical Classicism. It is the foundation stone of sound technique. Regardie's psychological insights and experienced advice are invaluable to the student. A further notable factor is the last volume on Enochian Magic.

This, it may be remembered, is the ultimate synthesis of all that has gone before and to which the Adepts were introduced. However, the Inner Order curriculum demands so much work that very few Adepts even reached the stage of elementary grappling with the Enochian System until Crowley turned his attention to the matter and explored the Thirty Aethyrs as recorded in *The Vision and the Voice*. Although this has yet to be surpassed, much work on the Enochian system was subsequently done by Regardie.The Enochian system , as we have noted, derives from the sixteenth-century angel magic of Dr John Dee and Edward Kelley. Here is the essence of the matter:

1 In a way which is still not quite clear, Dee and Kelley obtained 100 squares filled with letters and usually numbering 49 × 49.
2 Dee would have one or more of these squares before him.
3 Kelley sat at the Holy Table made according to angelic instruction and gazed at the shewstone, after a time seeing

an angel who would point with a rod to letters in succession on one of these charts.

4 Kelley would report, for instance: 'He points to column 5, rank 23,' apparently not mentioning the letter, which Dee found and wrote down from the square before him.

5 This implies that Kelley had absolutely no idea which words would be formed. To execute that feat, the man commonly denounced as a confidence trickster would have to have known the exact positions of the 2,401 letters in each of the tables. There must be an easier way of getting a living.

6 Angels dictated the words backwards, warning that undesired forces could be evoked by pronouncing them the right way.

7 Dee and Kelley rewrote the words forwards and the result was the Enochian Keys or Calls.

8 There are nineteen. The first two conjure the Element called Spirit; the next sixteen invoke the Four Elements, each sub-divided into four; and the nineteenth, by changing two names, can be used to invoke any one of Thirty 'Aethyrs', 'Aires', or dimensions of existence.

9 The language in which these Keys are written possesses a vocabulary, grammar and syntax of its own.

10 All of which leaves sceptics and subjectivists with a genuine and interesting intellectual problem:

(a) 'Enochian' bears virtually no relation to any known language;

(b) Yet philologists agree that it is impossible for a human being to invent a new language independently of known languages.

There are other issues too. The beauty of the Enochian keys is apparent in English translation. As Crowley writes in *The Confessions*:

> To condemn Kelley as a cheating charlatan – the accepted view – is simply stupid. If he invented Enochian and composed this superb

prose, he was at worst a Chatterton with fifty times that poet's ingenuity and five hundred times his poetical genius ... The genuineness of these Keys is guaranteed by the fact that anyone with the smallest capacity for Magick finds that they work.

The Complete Golden Dawn System of Magic contains a laudable essay by Dr Thomas Head which states: 'the most substantial and convincing proof of the *essential genuineness of both Dee and Kelley is their monumental ignorance of what to do with the material they have accumulated.*'

This was a favourite point of Regardie. In his view, it was the work of Mathers that was responsible for transforming the essence of a great mass of raw material into a practical system. This was the form in which Regardie himself pursued his researches. His practical experimentation enabled him to incorporate Enochian formulae in the rituals of self-initiation he called Opening by Watchtower, one of his major contributions to the science and art of Magic. He investigated the pronunciation and vocabulary of Enochian. He became one of the very few individuals who can play a complex game which summarizes one's understanding of the Golden Dawn system, Enochian Chess.

In his footnotes to Regardie's 1938 *Introduction To The Enochian System*, reprinted by Llewellyn Publications in their 5th edition of *The Golden Dawn*, Hal Sundt takes Regardie to task:

Israel Regardie was a member of Hermese [*sic*] Lodge for only a brief time in the 1930's, his main magical tutelage being with Crowley years *prior* to his admission to the G.D. The Hermes Lodge ... was a third generation G.D. temple which likely never inherited much of the oral materials and private papers of the original Mathers–Farr–Yeats Golden Dawn ... (Unfortunately, it is also mis-information and no credit to the late Israel Regardie). First, the original system of Dee and Kelley was vastly more sophisticated than even the Golden Dawn version, but it had not been pulled together at this time, so Regardie had insufficient materials at hand to form his judgement. Second, the Golden Dawn reduces all occult symbology to an

'Elemental Bias', and then combines elemental attributions quite mechanically to constitute everything into what they took of the Dee System. *This is valid and powerful*! 'for Dee', or 'for Mathers' to the discredit of the other really understand neither ... Unfortunately, Israel Regardie overlooked *Spirits and Apparitions*, Dee's published journals where pronunciation keys are given. Regardie's rendering of the Calls blurs pronunciation aids and Enochian spellings, a misguidance he inherited.

One can agree with Mr Sundt that there is much raw material left to us by Dee and Kelley which was not incorporated into the Golden Dawn system. Otherwise one is puzzled by a number of his statements. Firstly, although Regardie was indeed only a member of the Stella Matutina for a relatively short time, his studies and magical work enabled him to climb the Grades quickly to Adeptus Minor and so have access to all relevant documents. Secondly, his main *practical* magical tutelage wasn't with Crowley at all and we have noted his immense disappointment at the fact: Regardie – and this fact is of vital importance to all aspirants – was fundamentally self-educated; or perhaps we should say self-taught. Thirdly, Mr Sundt states that the Hermes Lodge 'likely never inherited much of the oral materials and private papers' of the original Golden Dawn. To which oral materials and private papers is Mr Sundt referring? One wishes that he could produce at least some scrap of evidence to support his contention. Instead he only offers the word 'likely'.

Fourthly, the 'mis-information' to which Mr Sundt refers is contained in the following words of Regardie:

Whoever was responsible for the Order scheme of the Angelic Tablets – whether it was Mathers and Westcott or the German Rosicrucian Adepts from whom the former are supposed to have obtained their knowledge – was possessed of an ingenuity and an understanding of Magic such as never was in the possession of Dee of Kelley.

Mr Sundt states baldly that the original Dee-Kelley system

was 'vastly more sophisticated than even the Golden Dawn version' but offers nothing to support his view. One learns with some surprise that this allegedly vastly sophisticated system of Dee and Kelley 'had not been pulled together at this time' which implies that at a later time, some individual researcher or group did indeed pull the matter together: but Mr Sundt responds to one's natural sense of enquiry by keeping the reader wholly in the dark.

Fifthly, we are informed that 'the Golden Dawn reduces all occult symbology to an 'Elemental Bias': one wonders where the 'bias' enters into the matter. The Golden Dawn simply went with the ancient magical tradition which affirms that all phenomena can be classified under the schema known as 'the Elements': to call that 'bias' is like insisting that chemists are 'biased' in their use of the Periodic Table. Obviously this work of classification is done, to use Mr Sundt's words, 'quite mechanically': how else would one do it?

There follows a bizarre statement made by Mr Sundt:

> *This is valid and powerful!* 'for Dee' or 'for Mathers' to the discredit of the other really understand neither.

What is Mr Sundt trying to tell us here? Lack of basic grammar interferes with meaning and any consequent weighing of his words. Why the inverted commas? What extra meaning do they possess? Perhaps Mr Sundt is attempting to tell us that ... It is really very hard to extract any logical meaning.

Tentatively I suggest the following translation, all the while painfully conscious that the meaning intended by Mr Sundt may be suffering a gross injustice. Apparently Dee and Mathers did themselves discredit by not understanding the Enochian System but despite this, it remained '*valid and powerful*!' for them. This begs two questions: (a) Is Mr Sundt claiming that he understands the Enochian System far better than Dee and Mathers – and Regardie? – and if so, how so and where is his evidence? And (b) Does Mr Sundt genuinely believe that one can misunderstand a magical system yet despite this it nevertheless remains '*valid and powerful*!' for oneself? I think we should be told.

In the seventh instance, Mr Sundt cites Dee's published journals which he terms *Spirits and Apparitions*. Despite the many months of arduous research the present writer undertook at the British Library in the course of editing, introducing and commenting upon *John Dee: Essential Readings* (1986), he is not familiar with any such title. Possibly Mr Sundt is citing an American title of the work: *A True & Faithful Relation of what passed for many years Between Dr. John Dee ... and Some Spirits*, edited by Meric Casaubon, published London 1659 and reprinted London 1976: but this was a text with which Regardie was perfectly familiar.

Finally, Regardie is criticized for his inherited misguidance regarding his poor spelling and pronunciation. He was of course guided in these matters by Crowley and the Golden Dawn/Stella Matutina: and more importantly, by years of experimentation in an endeavour to discover what worked. One would like to know where Mr Sundt obtained his true guidance and also his record of practical experimentation before one can take his unsupported assertions with any degree of serious consideration.

I apologize for what may have struck some as being a superfluous digression. Such was not the intention. It is surely germane to stress that Regardie knew precisely what he was writing about. His claims were modest. Here and there he may well have been mistaken and he freely admitted that possibility. Unfortunately, the same cannot be said for commentators such as Mr Sundt, who is clearly capable of making so many errors and begging so many questions in so very few ill-chosen words. One wishes that Mr Sundt had exercised more thought and care in his vainglorious phrases and that his publishers had inspected them more closely. As the matter stands, it serves to remind the student that in the reading of any magical treatise and as Regardie was fond of quoting, the old adage that: 'The First Virtue on the Path is Discrimination.'

Volume 10 of *The Complete Golden Dawn System of Magic* contains the Enochian System, skilled comment by working colleagues, the fruits of Regardie's own labours and his Enochian-English/English-Enochian dictionary. A beautiful, noble and efficacious system is at the disposal of those who want all of it and those who want some of it. All students owe to Regardie a great debt of gratitude, both for his early courage in breaking his oath of secrecy to a moribund collection of self-important loafers and for his later persistence in revising the material as a gift to the strange, wild and allegedly dangerous, who are the major hope of human evolution. The words of the Introduction he had written in his youth remain valid today:

It is for this reason that I hold that the Golden Dawn magic, the technique of initiation, is of supreme and inestimable importance to mankind at large. In it the work of academic psychology may find a logical conclusion and fruition, so that it may develop its own particular contribution to modern life and culture. For this psycho-magical technique of ceremonial initiation indicates the solution of the 'anima' problem.

'Arise! Shine! For thy light is come!'

Notes

1 Christopher Hyatt, Foreword to *What You Should Know about the Golden Dawn*.

2 Ibid.

3 Ibid.

4 Certain criticisms can be made. For example, the instructions for the performance of the Rose-Cross Ritual are turgid and unclear. One wishes that Regardie had revised or rewritten this early manuscript. But this is a minor blemish on a masterpiece.

The original *The Golden Dawn* has also been reprinted recently (1986) by Llewellyn Publications.

14

The Sage of Sedona

'Do what thou wilt shall be the whole of the Law.'

It was with these words that Dr Francis Israel Regardie stepped over the threshold of my West Hollywood apartment in autumn 1981. I had not seen him for nine years. It had been fifteen years since our initial contact.

I first encountered Regardie in 1966 at the age of fifteen through buying and reading one of his books. I was motivated then and still am now by a quest for Truth which had taken and would take many forms. In the course of this search I discovered that there was a non-sectarian, pre-Christian, Western mystical tradition. It was called Magic. There was only one problem: how to do it. The majority of authors on the subject either had no practical experience whatsoever; or else they eked out a little knowledge with dark hints about forbidden secrets and information on meditation which could be found in dozens of similar volumes, frequently adding insult to injury by hectoring one in tones which recalled a minor public school junior housemaster. It was therefore a relief to come upon the works of Aleister Crowley and to discover, after thorough research, that his evil legend was a mish-mash of lies, ignorance and malicious vilification. Here and at last was the real thing. I tried some of the practices he recommended and was pleased with the results. It was a relief too to meet Regardie in print. Common sense and clarity abounded in his writings. A week after buying one of his books, I bought two more. I started to work at the exercises he recommended and was delighted by the effects.

At this time I had absolutely no idea that there existed even the slightest connection between Regardie and Crowley. If one wanted Crowley's books, one had to go out and hunt for them in obscure specialist bookshops, often enduring wary glances, pitying looks and the odd dire warning from the booksellers. Regardie's works were much more readily available and even advertised in enthusiastically written leaflets issued by a respected book service of that time. People seemed to think that Crowley's works were dangerous, that he was so evil he had booby-trapped the rituals, that too much Crowley would drive one insane. Regardie, it appeared, was kosher. The Doctor was good for you. You were in safe hands there. I pictured Regardie as an elderly, learned and stern but benevolent Jewish Patriarch.

It was therefore astonishing to discover that this man had been secretary to The Beast 666 and had written a book about him, shortly to be published as *The Eye in the Triangle*. I sent a cheque in immediately and received the book about eighteen months later. I remember how excited I was when it finally arrived, preceded by many apologies for the publisher's delay from the book service. Here was one author whom I really respected writing on another whom I loved. I was deeply dissatisfied with all the works on Crowley I had scrutinized and had resolved to write the best one myself: an easy task in view of the competition then in being. Had Regardie written so judiciously, wisely and well as to render any subsequent efforts completely redundant?

I thought that the work was magnificent, though some questions still remained and their study prompted me to write to Dr Regardie care of his publishers. My letter praised his book warmly but raised a number of points to which he replied on 8 November 1971.

> I am happy to hear you are going to work on a book about Crowley [he wrote]. A writer visited me ten days ago, and will be in England next Spring to visit Gerald Yorke, and she too is at work on a book about Crowley, the man ... not the magician. The more the merrier.

He defended his decision to stop at 1914 with *The Eye*, answered queries on Sex Magick and the Devil, stated his criticisms of Anton LaVey's Church of Satan and gave all the information for which I'd asked on the fates of various individuals who had known Crowley. I'd enquired after a rumour spread about The Beast by the thriller writer Dennis Wheatley in *To the Devil – a Daughter*, that he had invoked Pan in Paris during the 1920s and it had sent him insane for six months. Suddenly Regardie's scholarly tone slipped delightfully:

I think Dennis Wheatley is nuts! That is not good psychology, philosophy nor anything else but expresses what I feel about his brand of nonsense.

Rewarding correspondence continued until summer 1972 when I was visiting California and Regardie invited me to come and see him. I was so keen not to be late that I arrived in his street an hour before the appointed time and had to park the car round the corner and walk impatiently up and down side-roads. I really didn't know what he'd be like in person, I wanted to make a good impression and I felt shy. Eventually I decided to do the Middle Pillar as I walked . . .

'Jesus, I had no idea you were so young,' he said as his door opened to me. He was a short, spry, balding man of slight build but obvious vigour. 'Well, come in and have a drink,' he added cheerfully, ushering me through a spacious, tastefully furnished and very comfortable house to his private bar. He walked with a spring and a bounce in his step. I asked for a whisky and he gave me a large one. 'Bet you can't have that in England,' he remarked jovially. When I told him I'd been enjoying whisky since the age of fifteen, he looked momentarily thoughtful and said: 'God, the place must've changed.'

He took me out to an excellent local steak-house and entertained me royally. He seemed much more interested in my words than in his, and I was nervous and appreciative of his attention. He was a charming dinner companion and he put me at my ease. Yes, of course Magic works and no, he couldn't stand cranks. 'For instance,' he said, in a unique tenor which mingled the accents of Mile End with those of the West Coast,

'I had a man ring me up the other day. Rang me from Manchester, reversed the charges if you please. He told me he was being *magically attacked*. Can you believe it? Oh, and a whole cock-and-bull story followed that. The man didn't realize that you *can't* be magically attacked unless you *want* to be magically attacked. The people who didn't like what I did in England during the Thirties – Inepti I call them – threw so many curses at me, I could've papered my walls with them; that was about all they were good for. Magically attacked – schmagically attacked – bah! – I got no use for that kind of adolescent gripe-water.'

He listened to my aspirations spiritual and material and offered sagacious advice. No, he definitely didn't recommend becoming an author unless I didn't mind being broke most of the time. Common sense urged that I should have a profession or trade so that whatever else I did, there'd always be a roof over my head, a bed to lie on and food to fill my belly. 'Any money I ever earned from my books couldn't keep anyone going for long. These days anything I get is just the frosting on the cake, financially speaking,' he observed. 'What writer can get a good living out of books?'

He affirmed certain truths of Magic and Mysticism, being so sensible and articulate about it all that I asked him why he didn't make efforts to publicize his message on the mass media. 'God forbid!' he exclaimed. 'The authorities would be down on me like a ton of bricks. Look what's happened to Timothy Leary.' Leary had only just been sentenced to ten years' imprisonment for possessing a tiny quantity of marijuana. 'No, no, I much prefer to steer well clear of the public eye.' He gave me names and addresses of correspondents in England who might prove helpful to me. A few years later, after Cambridge University and through circuitous routes, I would meet them all. Regardie and I parted that night with much expression of goodwill on either side. Afterwards I wrote him a thank you letter.

Although we had spoken much about Crowley, he seemed to think I was much too young to write on the subject. Here he was right, for my *Legacy of the Beast* wasn't written until 1986–7. I had the uncomfortable impression that I hadn't struck him as being anything more than a polite, well-intentioned and academically gifted kid. Here I was right, for as he wrote to me ten years later: 'I met you all those years ago. Nice, but not mind-blowing.' Moreover, he had somehow given me the impression that much as he revered the truths of Magic, its practice was part of his past, which disappointed me. Here I was wrong. As he would tell me years later, he deliberately gave that impression to everyone he met for the first time and to many for years afterwards. In any event, much as I had liked him and been thrilled to meet him, I did not pursue our correspondence and nor did he.

Years passed and with them many vicissitudes of fortune. In spring 1981, my then wife Ann and I went to live in West Hollywood, Los Angeles. There I learned that Regardie had recently moved to Sedona. I wanted to contact him again. Beginning my letter: 'Although you probably don't remember me . . .' I sent him one of my books in gratitude for his kindness all those years ago and in appreciation of his own works, which had done so much for me. He replied that of course he remembered me and many thanks for the book. He still visited LA sometimes . . . we wrote and invited him to lunch, which is how he came to be proclaiming the Law of Thelema in our apartment.

The occasion was a delight. At seventy-four, his vim and vigour put many young men to shame. He thought nothing of the ten-hour drive from Arizona to the West Coast through the Mojave desert. He was full of praise for our choice of restaurant, my books and life generally. Yet there was no talk of Magic. Instead we discussed psychology and psychoanalysis. At the end of the lunch he invited us for a weekend at his home some time. It took a while to finalize the details. His third marriage was breaking up, though we knew nothing of that at the time. Then he visited England for a friend's party at the Savoy. He may have enjoyed the occasion but he did not enjoy the rest of his time in the country of his birth, ringing me up on his return to exclaim: 'Terrible! Miserable! It's as bad as ever!'

'Don't mind me, I'm just a funny old man,' he informed us on our eventual arrival at his home. Then: 'You must be thirsty after your long drive. Would you like juice? Or would you prefer Christians?' His house, which looked out onto great red rocks and breathtaking canyons, consisted of two self-contained storeys. The upper floor was luxuriously furnished in the Western American style and adorned by strange and exquisite paintings and ornaments. The lower floor, where he slept and worked was book-lined and spacious and spartan.

'I had it built like this because I got married for the third time when I left Los Angeles,' he told us. 'You know, for fourteen years before we were married, we had a wonderful relationship. Probably it was because we didn't live together. I bought her an apartment. We used to spend every weekend together and once a week I'd take her out to dinner. So when we came here, I thought it'd work out if we had two totally self-contained spaces, different front doors, even. Well, we should've had at least a street between us.' A smile that was rueful and also regretful. 'The marriage lasted just eight months before she left.'

On the first night, he took us out to the best restaurant in town and gave extra entertainment by correctly guessing the astrological Sun Sign of ourselves, the manager, the waitresses and a number of other diners who had overheard and asked to be included. Later Ann spoke about a neck problem which had given her pain for many years, despite various treatments, and he put it right within a minute that very night.

Over the weekend he was a marvellous host, cooking with aplomb, playing Mozart's symphonies and spouting snatches of Romantic poetry. However, he did not share our taste for rock. 'Elvis Presley stuff? No way. D'you call that music?' His love of animals was evident in his devotion to his cat Leda; he said that some years before, he had bred English bulldogs. Magic was discussed only when I brought it up, and that was to explain that I hadn't done any in quite a while and to voice my disgust at the common run of occultists.

'Times haven't changed,' he shrugged. 'Well, I don't suppose it matters that you haven't done much lately. Sometimes there's just a period of lying fallow.' The subject of talismans came up. It will be remembered that these are objects which the Magician makes for the accomplishment of a specific aim and then charges by meditative (Middle Pillar) or ceremonial methods. If the objective is attained within seven days, the Magician claims that the talisman had worked.

'It's different when it comes to money, though,' I said.

'How d'you mean?' the old man queried.

'Well, every Magician with whom I've ever spoken says the same thing and it's true too in my own experience, that if the talisman is properly charged, you get just enough to avert disaster and tide you over and not one penny more.'

'Can't agree,' he responded flatly. 'Then you and everybody else must be doing something wrong.' And he related the tale of one of his talismans. 'Back in LA when I was in practice, I was doing quite well, earning on average around eighty thousand dollars a year. Trouble was that I spent it all as fast as I earned it. I'd more or less resigned myself to having to work until I kicked the bucket, except that I was getting older and finding it all a bit tiring. So I made a talisman for a great sum.

'Within a week, one of my patients whose treatment was ending made me a curious offer out of the blue. He said that I'd done a lot for him and now he wanted to do his bit for me. He was a successful investment consultant and he suggested that I placed any savings I had with him for a market killing that was coming. Well, I did that, and I must admit I had grave doubts about the wisdom of that action because whenever I'd done anything like it in the past, I'd always lost money and I'm probably the world's worst investor. Anyway, my friend put all my money into silver just before the Hunt family tried to corner the market. The result was that I could cash in my chips and retire out here.'

We argued about the origins of the Golden Dawn. At that time, I accepted Ellic Howe's proof that the Order was indeed founded on a fraud by Dr Westcott: but I didn't think it mattered; it was the techniques which were all-important. Regardie was convinced that no fraud had been committed and that the Order had the origin it claimed – which was Continental and Rosicrucian. He produced in evidence a photograph of Westcott, aptly described by Ithell Colqhoun as 'a darling old pussy cat of a man'. 'Does he look to you like the sort of man who would commit fraud?' Regardie demanded. 'They never do,' Ann replied. Argument had to become more scholarly and did. Regardie urged that I study the matter in greater depth and invited me to conribute an essay on the matter to the forthcoming edition of *What You Should Know about the Golden Dawn*. It would be written and published as *Suster's Answer to Howe*.

From that time onward, I was in regular contact with Regardie, in person, via correspondence and on the phone. I returned to his home. His energy remained remarkable for a man his age. After a six-hour round trip by car to and from Phoenix Airport to pick me up, all he needed was the sixty-minute nap he took from five till six every day. Then he'd wander into the kitchen, make himself one of the two cocktails with which he began his evenings – there'd be nothing more later except the occasional glass of wine with dinner – and he'd exclaim heartily: 'Thank God for booze!' His mind was continually active and alert. Occasionally he would forget a name or a date, which would infuriate him. He'd slap his face and exclaim irritably: 'God damn you, Regardie, you're going senile!' Nothing could have been further from the truth.

His infectious good humour affected everyone around him. Even when his frequent jokes weren't that funny, they were told with such gusto that one still laughed anyway. A steady stream of visitors came and went. It was good to see that even at his advanced age, his amorous activities continued unabated. One thinks too of the married woman who had been a patient of his a few years ago and who rang him from LA in terror of an impending nervous breakdown: her husband had left her and she had no money. The old man paid for her trip to stay a couple of days with him for treatment, which was free of charge and an unprecedented event in the American medical profession. When she arrived, she'd looked fit for suicide in a parking lot but she left smiling and visibly determined. 'Hope to God I've done something for her,' Regardie muttered.

His charming daily help could not accept that since he was Doctor Regardie and since he was known to heal people, he was nevertheless not a medical doctor. She kept asking for his advice and remedies for all her ailments and those of her family. It was no use Regardie telling her that he was not a doctor. As far as she was concerned, he was *Doctor* Regardie and so he must know best. In time, Regardie realized that it couldn't be helped and so prescribed his unique remedies for colds, flu and sinus infection, sore throats, coughs, indigestion and other common ills, invariably recommended products which could be bought without a prescription in any drug store but adding some special process which sounded miraculously scientific to the less lettered ear. 'You see, Mrs X,' he'd declare wisely, 'I've always been a great believer in *old fashioned* remedies'. Instantly Mrs X would look safe and secure. 'The *old fashioned* ones are the best in my experience, believe me. Now: what I'm recommending strongly for your mother's problem is aspirin. Good, plain, old-fashioned aspirin. And you take it with hot blackcurrant juice. BUT there is one *absolutely vital* point where far too many people go wrong. The hot water you pour on the blackcurrant juice concentrate *must not be boiling*. All right? *At no time* can it be allowed to boil. Very important. You know what happens if you pour boiling water on the blackcurrant juice? Ruins it. It kills the Vitamin C.' It remains only to be added that the lady in question thought that Regardie was a wonderful doctor whose cures she swore by because they always worked.

His house was Liberty Hall, a glorious vision of sunlight, good cheer and creativity. He was working on a book; so was I; and it was easy to disappear into a space where one wouldn't be disturbed. Evenings were sometimes enlivened by convivial dinner parties he gave for his neighbours. There was a good word for almost everyone he encountered in Sedona, where he seemed to be known and popular. He was a man who loved life. He booked a friend, himself and myself on the local jeep trip round the canyons one time, in which the vehicle zoomed up and down crazy hillocks at angles of up to seventy degrees, rather like a roller coaster, and he laughed uproariously while we shrieked; it was his fifth time. Even when he didn't care for a particular pleasure, he always sounded regretful about the fact. 'I wish I liked beer,' he sighed as he saw me quaff a stein of German lager. 'The people who drink it seem to get so much enjoyment from the stuff.'

But there was dedication beneath the comedy. You had to badger him in order to find it but once cornered, he became serious. Not that he ever tried coming on like a Master or even an Adept. 'I'm a student. We're all students,' he insisted, 'and if anybody says he's no longer a student, I'd like to meet him.' Few things irritated him more than the fatuous hunt for gurus or invisible guides onto whom the aspirant pours his problems while enjoying a masturbatory ego-rub for his depth of spiritual insight. 'The true Master is within you,' he urged, 'do it yourself.'

I must've driven him mad with my questions. When I didn't like his answers I argued with him and he argued back. Sometimes these sessions would climax in going through a sacred text, line by line and word by word. Since everyone who knew him praised his divinatory skills, I persuaded him to supervise my ritual work. Earlier, I had seen him work a ceremony of his own.

There was a Temple tucked away on the lower floor. The door was always kept locked. Within, there was a windowless room with an altar at the centre. Upon this altar there reposed a candle for Fire, a Chalice of wine for Water, a rose for Air and a dish of bread and salt for Earth – the Magician's Eucharist of the Four Elements in which the gods indwell when successfully invoked. The four walls had just the four Enochian

Elemental Tablets. Regardie wore white: a fellow-initiate and I were robed in black. He sat us down in chairs at opposite ends of the Temple, for our role on this occasion was simply to be present and aware, and taking up a beautifully crafted Lotus Wand, he commenced the ritual of Opening by Watchtower by which, among other things, the powers of the Four Elements are conjured.

One's mood at the start of serious magical work is sometimes sceptical and sullen, paradoxically enough. One's initial desire to do it is without warning succeeded by a hundred reasons for not doing it or putting it off until tomorrow. One wonders why on earth one is doing it: it suddenly strikes one as being all a bit silly. And I confess that this was my mood as Regardie started work. There was a sense of nervous irritation and overwhelming inertia. It occurred to me to wonder idly what the hell I was doing sitting here like a fool in some peculiar room with a funny old man. At that time, I was going through periods of accepting, from experience, that Magic worked, but questioning the point of it; and I had attended some rituals which frankly bored me. So the oration from Zoroaster's *Chaldean Oracles*: 'Stoop not down into that darkly splendid world wherein continually lieth a faithless depth and Hades wrapped in gloom, delighting in unintelligible images, precipitous, winding; a black ever-rolling abyss, ever espousing a body unluminous, formless and void' left me unmoved. Slowly though, I became conscious of the unmistakable fact that something odd was happening as Regardie conjured Fire. No, it couldn't be my imagination. I was definitely starting to feel uncomfortably hot.

And when, after all the phantoms have vanished, thou shalt see that holy and formless fire, that fire which darts and flashes through the hidden depths of the Universe, hear thou the Voice of Fire ... OIP TEAA PEDOGE. In the names and letters of the Great Southern Quadrangle, I invoke ye, ye Angels of the Watchtower of the South.

I had never known anything like the sensation I was experiencing. It was as though I was sitting in an oven which was getting hotter. Perspiration poured down my face and landed in big droplets on my robe and on the floor – I wasn't sweating so much as pouring with rain. It was very difficult to breathe. There was fire in my cells and it hurt, my throat was parched, I was gasping for air and I feared I might pass out from the searing heat.

So therefore first, the priest who governeth the works of fire must sprinkle with the lustral water of the loud resounding sea . . . EMPEH ARSEL GAIOL. In the names and letters of the Great Western Quadrangle, I invoke ye, ye Angels of the Watchtower of the West.

As he chanted the invocation of Water, I felt that if I did not have water to quench my thirst and cool my inflamed skin, I might expire. He sprinkled from the Chalice at that point and I screamed inwardly for moisture. A few drops landed on my bare arms, then appeared to expire in steam. Simultaneously there was a downpour of sweat from my brow and all the fluids of my bowels stirred and slopped about.

Such a fire existeth, extended through the rushing of Air. Or even a fire formless, whence cometh the image of a voice. Or even a flashing light, abounding, revolving, whirling forth, crying aloud . . . ORO IBAH AOZPI. In the names and letters of the Great Eastern Quadrangle, I invoke ye, ye Angels of the Watchtower of the East.

With the conjuration of Air, there was a blowing of a hot, dry wind within the room. It was as though he had turned on a heater which remorselessly blasted out the mid-day desert air. Perspiration dried upon me. Gases rumbled within my belly. Never in my life had I felt so physically weak, my brain whirled and in my ears there was a humming. I couldn't breathe in the stifling air. I fought the temptation to collapse on the floor in an unconscious heap.

EMOR DIAL HECTEGA. In the names and letters of the Great Northern Quadrangle, I invoke ye, ye Angels of the Watchtower of the North.

I was beyond any kind of response to the invocation of Earth. I just sat there like a stone dummy, relieved that I hadn't collapsed; though once this was over, I intended to flop down on my bed and lie prone for many hours. When the ceremony ended, I wasn't sure if I could rise from my chair but somehow I made it and managed to stagger out of the room.

There was a period in the lavatory then I sagged onto the bed. To my surprise, strength started to return within just a few minutes. It wasn't long before I rose easily and went to see the others in the kitchen. My Golden Dawn colleague asked concernedly if I was all right. She'd noticed that I'd been perspiring furiously and wondered why. I told them exactly why.

'Were you frying my fat or something?' I asked Regardie.

'Curious,' was all he would say. And a day later I went through precisely the same ritual without any ill effects at all and came out wholly invigorated. That was true too of all subsequent Temple work and teaching.

There is a letter of his which I unashamedly treasure. I had written to him after an April visit thanking him for his hospitality and expressing the hope that we would become friends. His letter of 7 May 1982 stated: 'we are (not will be) friends.' He had many friends; I was just one of them. Our friendship was that which obtains between two men who value truth above all else, when one is young and fiery and the other is old and wise. My respect and affection for 'the old man' are obvious, though they never interfered with the expression of my own views whenever they differed from those of Regardie and I treasure the memory also of our long, detailed and cordial arguments. My enthusiasm for his work never interfered with intellectual criticism or the voicing of insights I was eager to test against his own views.

On evenings when there were just the two of us, Regardie

and I would sit out on the deck which surrounded his home and gaze across at the dark canyons and up at the stars. Sometimes I'd ask him more questions. How did he feel, for instance, about the publication of early works of his with which he now disagreed? He replied that he had no right to censor the earnest work of a much younger man. On another occasion, I enquired after the people who had personally influenced his life most. He told me there were four, three women and one man. He declined to name two of the women, save to state that they were not his wives, and as has been noted, one was Maria de Miramar. The man, of course, was Crowley.

I recall one dinner-party when there was plenty of wine and cognac and hash cookies and I became excessively vibrant – one would certainly term it 'over the top' – and startled some of the guests. The following midday I wandered into the dining-room looking and feeling hungover. Regardie was having lunch. 'You know who you were last night?' he said cheerfully; 'The Imp Crowley. Not the Master Therion. The Imp Crowley.'

We had one passion in common besides the concerns of this book, of the arts and sciences or our love of life: boxing. Every Thursday evening, Regardie used to watch television, the only time I ever saw him do that. This was solely because Thursday night was one TV station's 'Fight Night' and there was a very good programme for all boxing fans, *Tomorrow's Champions*. On 15 December 1983, he would write to me: 'I think of you often – especially on Thursday nights when I watch the boxing on TV. I still find it interesting; works off a lot of my own latent tensions as if I were in the ring myself.'

I learned much from him which I still cannot put into words. But I clearly recall one curious conversation. We were sitting out beneath the stars and I'd just told him some true story in which I was convinced I'd acted honourably – and yet by conventional standards behaved outrageously. This was on my last visit, shortly before my return to England.

'You have the nerve of the Devil,' he said and he chuckled away, then suddenly a sadness passed over his face. 'Good luck in England. Buggered if I know why you like it so much – I never did. I'm truly sorry you've decided to leave God's own country to return to dear old Blighty. But there it is; if you've decided, so be it. I really am not at all sure you'll like it when you return. It won't be easy. My intuition tells me it won't all go as well as you hope. There'll be problems and quite a number of them.'

I thought of the pains I'd suffered in America – among other things, my marriage had broken up – and of further pains I might have to endure on my return and these thoughts weren't comforting, though on this night I was braced for the future. After a pause I said: 'Something I wanted to ask you. Don't you reckon that the gods and goddesses are ultimately just a bunch of celestial gangsters and their molls – as Homer pointed out?'

'Yes,' he responded thoughtfully, 'yes, there's truth in that. Not All Truth, but it's one way of looking at it. Homer saw it, so did Shakespeare: "As flies are we to the wanton gods, they kill us for their sport..." But unless you've been singled out for that – and you haven't because they pick 'em young and bless them with everything before they top them – and that hasn't happened to you – the general rule is that you never go to the wall as long as you're doing the gods' work. Now go to it!' he exclaimed and chuckled. 'And good luck and may the gods bless you.'

I returned to England and we carried on corresponding. His letters gave joy to my life. Sometimes he wrote in them views which he would not have wanted published under his name during his lifetime as when, in his letter of 8 December 1982, he discussed a certain private matter which affected both of us.

> Who the hell could have created such circumstances and worked out a whole set of gambits that would bring you together? I suggest that this is the working of the Gods, the Secret Chiefs, your Holy Guardian Angel or what-not. But certainly some praeter-human intelligence of some kind is involved here. I've seen this so many times, I am occasionally bowled over by the supreme brilliance of

their handling of so many diverse factors, so many different people and events in order to bring off some extraordinary event which ordinarily would pass unnoticed as just something that had happened ... Anyway, maybe you know what I'm talking about.

He sent me gifts of books which he had warmly inscribed to me. His letters made clear that he was still leading an active and stimulating life. In summer 1983 he travelled with a woman friend to Fiji, Australia and New Zealand for magical as well as personal reasons. In February 1984, he went to Hawaii with friends from the Falcon Press and wrote to me on 19 March:

Hawaii was lovely ... there were six of us. It is a perfectly beautiful set of islands (ruined of course by the Christian missionaries and now the scene of hostility between the native Polynesians and the white folk, the Japanese there being on the side of the whites). The weather is superb, warm the whole year round, lovely breezes constantly moving, the temperature just right - and ablaze with colour of flowers, reds, magentas and apricot - incredible. My chest functioned there a great deal better than most places, and that was why I decided to go there ... If all goes well, I may move there. That's still in the lap of the Gods.

There wasn't the slightest sign of senility in his letters, though as he grew older he became more and more impatient with wilful stupidity among authors on the occult. One was 'a silly arse and that's all there is to it'. Of another he wrote simply: 'He is a shit.' I found these pithy statements to be perfectly true on meeting the gentlemen in question. Gradually, however, there were darker notes of unhappiness peppering his generally cheerful and encouraging tone.

A couple of possible lawsuits are in the offing against which both I and Falcon must defend ourselves, that is if they come off. I am toying with the idea that once that threat is over, to employ all legal means to terminate my contracts which place me in someone's power. I don't like it one bit. In business matters I am such an idiot. I should never have got myself involved contractually and legally in this way. My only feeble excuse is that I thought I was dealing with friends, and friends would not coerce me. I was wrong (6 May 1984).

Things are lousy for the time being for both of us – and many more too. These aspects are far-reaching. So let me hope that shortly things will ease up and produce some better conditions for both of us (2 June 1984).

Then in a letter which thanked me warmly for two of my novels and 'some good reading time':

My mood continued; I didn't want to do any work. I have a lot to do. I have three mss. from a Golden Dawner in New Zealand which need to be severely edited, and have an Introduction written for them. But I just can't get down to work (18 June 1984).

Forgive my long silence. I have not been well. First of all I had surgery for a left inguinal hernia. After that I contracted some kind of viral infection, which laid me rather low. Not in the sense of really being ill, but mostly leaving me devoid of energy. I am still rather inert but I am on the way up, thank heaven ... Thanks for the birthday card ... this coming Saturday. 77 yrs of age, entering upon my 78 year. Hell – that's old! ... I hope things are beginning to pick up for you now. It has been a long haul. Saturn can be a pain in the arse all right. I've got two or three more months of its afflictions and then I hope things begin to improve. Same with you ... All the best, still feel inert but ... (13 November 1984).

This, the penultimate letter I received from Regardie, contained a request which returns us to the concerns expressed in the very first chapter of this work.

Can I impose on you and ask a favor? I am sure the British Museum has all the past issues of the *Occult Review*. Around 1932–33, I wrote a two part article for them entitled *A Jewish Mystical Movement* (about Chassidim), under the pseudonym of Yisroel ben Baruch ha-Chassid. If it doesn't inconvenience you too much, could you get me a Xeroxed copy of it for me? I'd appreciate it no end. And while you're doing it, around the same time I did a book review on a book entitled JESUS ... Getting hold of both of these would be a great favor. Whatever it costs, do let me know ... Just let me know and I'll send you some cash for it.

Obviously I sent him the materials he'd requested and received the last letter I ever had from him, which I quote in full:

Dear Gerald,

Thank you so very much for the copies of the stuff from the *Occult Review*. I do appreciate it tremendously. Now be a nice guy and let me know how much it cost you, and I'll send you some cash (not a check which costs something to cash in England) by return. Don't stand on ceremony about this. I do know what it's like to be hard up on occasion so ....

The Jesus review is interesting. I haven't got the book now, but I'll get Weiser's to try and pick up a copy here. I wrote the authors of *Holy Blood: Holy Grail* what would happen to their thesis (that Jesus was married and had off-spring) if they accepted the notion presented in Frank's (and many, many others) that there was no such beastie, but they haven't answered - nor do I think they will.

The Chassid article was interesting. Falcon want to include it in a book on Jewish topics to which some Jungians and other Jewish scholars are contributing.

I am amused by my article, for as you know Judaism and Christianity don't mean a thing to me. That article was written after Buber's book came out in England, and just after I discovered a Chassid schtubel in the East End, which intrigued me no end. But my article is so unlike me that I must conclude it was written either with tongue in cheek or was just plain hypocrisy.

I wanted then, and still do, an occultism without religious theology. Blavatsky's *Secret Doctrine* got me moving on that trail initially. And the thing that I cottoned onto with Crowley and the *Equinoxes* originally was the absence of any religious notion. It was only later, when he got bitten by the Liber AL, that the tone of his writing changed considerably, and it was no longer as exciting and vigorous as the first ten *Equinoxes*.

Anyway, it was interesting to get hold of some stuff written 50 years ago. It was contemporary with *The Garden of Pomegranates* and

The Tree of Life. I am glad they are without the Jewish Chassid viewpoint.

Anyway, that's that. Many thanks again for getting these copies made for me. I am highly appreciative. All the very best, Always, Francis (10 December 1984).

The ambivalence towards *The Book of the Law* remained to the end. It is surprising that Regardie did not observe that *The Equinox*, which he praises, followed directly on from Crowley's decision to accept *The Book of the Law* fully in 1909. Furthermore, we see at the end the issues of the beginning in the reaction of the prosperous Dr Regardie to the Judaism in which he had originally been reared.

The last communication I had from him contained the sum of money promised for photo-copying purposes. Then there was silence. I am told that during this time, his health deteriorated rapidly, much to his disgust. He had hoped for a long, peaceful life amidst beautiful surroundings once he had finished with *The Complete Golden Dawn System of Magic* – Jews customarily end service in Synagogue by shaking hands and saying: 'I wish you a long life.' It didn't seem that this would be the case. He had declared on many occasions too that death didn't frighten him, only senility, and since his faculties were at last beginning to degenerate, he announced his intention to die soon and reincarnate almost immediately afterwards.

On 11 March 1985 I received a phone-call from Los Angeles. The speaker was an old friend of his. She had been a patient, she had received some magical instruction, she had founded a Golden Dawn Temple in Los Angeles. Unfortunately, some quarrel had led to a parting with Regardie in 1983: but her grief was obvious. She told me that Francis was dead. He'd gone out to dinner with a man friend of many years, it had been a very good dinner – probably, and appropriately, at his favourite Sedona restaurant which was called The Owl – and over coffee, a massive heart attack had killed him.

It was the way he would've wanted to go, quickly and cleanly, and preferably after a good dinner. Another version of his death has been cited earlier (Chapter I): either way, it was the departure of a sage. Yet when I put the phone down, I grieved for a friend and ached for the loss; something good had gone out of this world.

His departure was mourned by all who had known him and the many who had read his works. His Will was characteristically simple. He left his money to his favourite nephew Arnold, a prosperous Los Angeles lawyer of whom Francis had often spoken fondly, and everything else to the Israel Regardie Foundation, set up and administered by Christopher Hyatt. The words of Dr Johnson on the tombstone of Oliver Goldsmith surely aply also to the life and work of Israel Regardie: 'He touched nothing that he did not adorn.'

My intention in this chapter and at various points throughout this work has been to show the informal side to a man who had learned to harmonize the joys and sorrows of life on this planet with the rapture of questing after the starry heavens. Some of Regardie's views are obviously open to question: for instance, few share his opinion, based on practical experience nevertheless, that Wilhelm Reich's 'Orgone Energy Accumulators' are of great mind-body benefit to anyone who tries them.

Francis Israel Regardie was no saint; the very idea would make him laugh. Nor was he a genius, though he recognized genius whenever and wherever he encountered it: and some might argue that in his later, specifically magical work, he was on occasion possessed by genius in a manner which surprised him. Leaving that aside, it can be said with certainty that he grew from very little to become a fine healer, an excellent author, a supreme exponent of both psychology and the Western Esoteric Tradition and one in whom wisdom ultimately reposed. Nor can I ever forget the warmth of his friendship and his noble generosity of purse, mind, heart, guts and soul.

Though I have criticized his work wherever I have found it

doubtful, I have no hesitation in stating that his attainments at the time I knew him were way ahead of any I may possess – I still have much catching up to do – and that he was, is and will be an enduring guide, philosopher and friend to all who hunger after the genuine truths of matter and spirit.

15

Ecce Homo

What did Francis Israel Regardie contribute to the sum of human knowledge and understanding? What, if anything, did he do to further the evolution of human consciousness?

One hopes that these questions have been answered fully by what has gone before: but perhaps a summary is necessary.

1 Regardie showed that an ordinary person hampered by socio-economic disadvantages of every kind can nevertheless attain to a satisfying material life while passionately pursuing the quest for sacred truths.
2 He brought together Magic and psychology as tools for the development of the whole Person. In so doing, he substantially broadened the scope of the magical tradition and supplied unique insights into the workings of the human psyche.
3 By his life and work he demonstrated the essential sanity of the Western Esoteric Tradition.
4 He remains by far the best guide to the demanding, advanced and complex issues tackled by Aleister Crowley.
5 His work on the Golden Dawn system augmented that body of knowledge, enabled it to survive and inspired its present revival.
6 His work was part of a general expansion of human consciousness beyond the despair of life as merely 'birth, copulation and death'. His short manuals maintained that we are not 'the hollow men, the stuffed men', and that there is something simple and practical which we can do here and now to remedy that despair.
7 In later life, regretting his youthful desire to impress with long words and cumbersome clauses, he wrote so as to make the complex simple and comprehensible: and

although he was painfully aware of the difficulties involved in any attempt to communicate metaphysical truths, he also taught the practical means by which these truths may be apprehended.

8 Regardie's body of work therefore gives the simplest enquirer access to wisdom and to various methods of realizing it within the Self, which methods are described in the plainest possible language. Those who follow these methods will certainly come to no harm and are far more likely to grow on all levels until they are fit vehicles for the reception of that Light - or L.V.X. (*lux*) - for which he sought so sincerely and which he found. Those who have a thorough grounding in Regardie's theories and praxis but who then go on to other ways, will have acquired a firm and fine foundation for that Temple of the Holy Spirit each one of us must eventually build.

9 He put together in his books a Way by which anyone with persistence can attain to mystical illumination, knowledge of one's True Will, expression of genuine emotion, full discerning functioning of intellect, free flow of sexuality, solid common sense and a balanced control of each harmonized faculty.

10 Finally, Regardie attained to an understanding of Magic and its Light, though his modesty often masked this. He could not express this understanding in the form of poetic utterance. He wrote in the Way of Truth rather than in the Way of Beauty, though as Keats pointed out, the two are ultimately one. The plain fact remains that he was for a time openly the supreme exponent of the Western Wisdom Tradition which is equal in every Way to the noble teachings of the East, which Ways are our only hope for the regeneration of this currently benighted planet.